THE FIREHOUSE **COOKBOOK**

Similar cookbooks from
Random House Value Publishing:

Are You Hungry Tonight? Elvis' Favorite Recipes
The Biker Cookbook
Campbell's Quick and Easy Recipes
The Country Music Cookbook
Recipes from Granny's Kitchen

THE
FIREHOUSE **COOKBOOK**

150 RECIPES FROM FIREHOUSES ALL OVER THE U.S.

DOROTHY JACKSON KITE

Illustrations by Nancy Tausek

GRAMERCY BOOKS
New York

This 2001 edition is published by Gramercy Books™, an imprint of Random House Value Publis
Inc. 280 Park Avenue, New York, N.Y. 10017 by arrangement with the author.

Gramercy Books™ and design are trademarks of Random House Value Publishing, Inc.

Random House
New York • Toronto • London • Sydney • Auckland
http://www.randomhouse.com/

Printed and bound in the United States of America

Library of Congress Cataloging-in-Publication Data

Kite, Dorothy Jackson, 1922-.
    The firehouse cookbook / Dorothy Jackson Kite ; illustrations by Nancy Tausek.
        p. cm.
    Reprint. Originally published: New York : Viking Press, 1975.
    Includes index.
    ISBN 0-517-21880-1
    1. Cookery, American. I. Title.

TX715 .K622 2001
641.5973--dc21

2001033027

9 8 7 6 5 4 3 2

THIS BOOK IS DEDICATED TO THE HONORABLE MEMBERS OF OUR SOCIETY WHO KEEP WATCH OVER OUR LIVES AND PROPERTY EVERY HOUR OF EVERY DAY—THE FIREFIGHTERS.

Contents

Preface

My main concern while compiling this cookbook has been the thought that some people might get the false idea that firefighters sit around the station cooking and eating all day long. The truth is that firefighters today work continually to keep abreast of our ever-changing society. Their job is the most hazardous in the nation and demands expert knowledge of many fields. It was because of the dedication of my husband and so many other firefighters throughout the country that I sought a way to help further the public relations of the fire service.

I knew very little about the technical aspects of firefighting, so I settled on food preparation as a subject of common interest that everyone could share. Because their job requires around-the-clock duty, most firemen cook and eat at the station. For a long time I have been interested in the recipes used at the firehouse kitchen in our city. But even though I have had years of cooking experience, I found myself increasingly intrigued as my husband related to me the basic, direct methods that characterize meal preparation at a firehouse. With three or four men working together on different recipes for the same meal, the firehouse system is not without its antics as well, and the stories are often as amusing as they are instructive.

My research into the methods employed in our own fire-department kitchen led me to the realization that there must be hundreds of adept chefs in firehouse kitchens all over the country, men with years of experience in the art of simple but effective kitchen procedures. I decided to mail out requests for their favorite recipes, and thus began the nationwide quest for the special fire-department recipes compiled in this cookbook.

Our first request went to Greenville, South Carolina. In a short while we received several recipes from Firefighter Dave Porter and Captain L. C. Garrett in Greenville with a heartening request of their own: "We would like to have one of your cookbooks whenever they are ready." I knew then that I had to get busy, and our venture grew from there.

I never intended to get in touch with every fire department in the country, as there are more than 25,000 of them. Because I had no preferences, I merely wrote fire departments in cities chosen at random from a map of the United States. I wish I had had the time to write to each fire department, paid and volunteer, in every city and also to the many fine county fire departments.

I have tried to use all the recipes I received and to preserve, as nearly as possible, the originality of each one. Where a particularly popular dish was prepared in a number of firehouse kitchens, I included several versions of the recipe to indicate its wide appeal, I found it interesting to try different versions from firehouses that were miles and miles apart. If two recipes were almost identical, I chose to use the one received first or the one that was a single submission from a firehouse kitchen.

You will notice there are two listings for ingredient amounts. Many recipes used by fire departments are intended for groups of men numbering ten, twelve, or more who have hearty appetites. Persons cooking for a smaller group, however, would not find these large amounts practical. No one should be presented with a mathematical problem for each ingredient in every recipe, so, for the sake of efficiency, I have a double listing.

Although the dishes served at firehouse tables run the gamut from wild geese to snapping turtles, from pigs' knuckles to plum cake, and from crab legs to cracklin' cornbread, the exotic will not often be found on the menu. The men on occasion splurge on costly fare, but realize that this type of diet on a steady basis would be a little ridiculous. They invariably prefer the foods most familiar to the average American. They prepare many foreign dishes so expertly that they could pass the test of the most prestigious gourmet, but, like most of us, firefighters must budget their money and time and will waste neither on elaborate, involved cuisine. Many dishes are of the type that requires a minimum of preparation time and can be left simmering or baking while the men go about their fire-related duties, which always have priority.

Italian foods are a favorite, especially spaghetti and pasta-with-meat casseroles. Some Chinese and Mexican dishes are often tried, and chili con carne is particularly popular. There are English, French, Hungarian, German, and Swedish recipes, but traditional down-to-earth American favorites—fried or baked chicken, steak smothered in onions, baked or fried fish, barbecued pork, juicy seasoned hamburgers, corn fritters, and macaroni and cheese—are menu items the firefighters find hard to beat. Firehouse-baked dinner rolls or steaming, buttered cornbread are often served with fresh vegetables or salads. Soups and stews of meats and vegetables simmered to perfection are frequent meal-pleasers in a single dish. The delicious desserts vary from homemade ice cream and fresh-baked apple or coconut pie to a rich banana pudding. None of this may be exotic, but it is "smacking" good food, tested in firehouse kitchens throughout the country by men and women who have turned a necessity into an enjoyable avocation.

Though this book deals with a secondary role at the fire station, I hope it will serve as an instrument of good will and reflect the spirit of confidence of the many fine men who have helped and encouraged us with this project.

You, the reader, will also become a discoverer, as I have, of the culinary abilities of these men as you journey through this book to the kitchens of firehouses throughout the country.

Acknowledgements

I wish to thank the personnel of all fire departments represented in this book for their participation in the project. Their involvement was essential for it provided the substance of the book. To those who added notes of encouragement in their correspondence, I give an extra "Thank you." From every section of the country came notes such as these: "I wish you every success with your endeavor." "Please keep us posted on your progress." "If we can be of any further help, please let us know." And often only two words, "Good luck."

The free spirit of assistance given to me in the writing and compiling of this cookbook only reaffirms a belief I had in the beginning—we are very fortunate in this country to be under the dedicated protection of so many fine persons in the fire service.

On the personal side, I would like to include an appreciative note to my family—my husband, Roy; daughter, Barbara; sons, Larry and Donald; and daughter-in-law, Donna, for assuming the roles of testers and tasters to help me with the difficult task of arriving at a selection of recipes from the many good ones submitted.

Concerning the reprint of The Firehouse Cookbook—some twenty-five years after its original publication—I want to thank my son-in-law and daughter, Joe and Barbara, for their insight and commitment toward this purpose. Ironic timing led them to work successfully with Nancy Davis and others at Random House Value Publishing who had also decided to pursue this same goal.

Many of the firefighting personnel named in this book have since retired from the fire service. Others are respectfully remembered for their contribution to the job of firefighting. All chose and held the honorable job of helping their fellow man.

DOROTHY JACKSON KITE
MARCH 2001

[FIREHOUSE RECIPES]

from the
New England
and
Middle Atlantic States

St. Clair
Italian Spaghetti

Italian spaghetti is as popular in the Lewiston, Maine, fire-house as it is in firehouse kitchens throughout the U.S.A. It ties for first place with another firefighter favorite—chili con carne.

SERVES 12	INGREDIENTS	SERVES 6
1 cup	Onions	½ cup
1 lb.	Ground beef	½ lb.
4 Tbs.	Olive oil	2 Tbs.
2 Tbs.	Butter or margarine	1 Tbs.
2	Garlic cloves	1
2 10¾-oz. cans	Tomato soup	1 10¾-oz. can
2 6-oz. cans	Tomato paste	1 6-oz. can
2 No. 2 cans	Tomatoes, drained	1 No. 2 can
2 10½-oz. cans	Beef broth	1 10½-oz. can
To taste	Salt and pepper	To taste
2 tsp.	Oregano	1 tsp.
1 Tbs.	Sugar	½ Tbs.

Spaghetti

Chop onions and garlic. Brown onions and ground beef in olive oil. Add butter, garlic, and remaining sauce ingredients. Simmer about two hours, until thickened, stirring occasionally. Skim off excess fat and serve over hot, cooked spaghetti.

Note: A whole raw potato can be added to absorb grease while sauce is simmering. It should be removed when soft.

COOK Maurice St. Clair   CHIEF Reginald A. Doucette, Jr.

Fish Chowder

This recipe for fish chowder—a New England specialty—was sent to us with the best compliments of the firehouse chef in Lewiston.

SERVES 12	INGREDIENTS	SERVES 6
6 to 8 ozs.	Salt pork	3 to 4 ozs.
4	Onions	2
8	Potatoes	4
2 qts.	Milk	1 qt.
2 lbs.	Fillet of haddock or other boned fish	1 lb.
To taste	Salt and pepper	To taste
4 Tbs.	Butter	2 Tbs.
	Paprika (optional)	

Dice salt pork and fry in skillet until brown. Remove pork and set aside. Add chopped onion to pork fat and cook until lightly brown being careful not to burn. Remove onions from pan and set aside to drain. Peel and thinly slice potatoes. Place in stewing pan, cover with water, and cook until almost done. Add milk, pork dice, and onions to potatoes, leaving potato water in pan for thickening. Add salt, pepper, and butter. Simmer—*do not boil.* Add fish (cut in bite-sized pieces) to stew for 15 minutes before you are ready to serve. Sprinkle with paprika, if desired, and serve with oyster crackers.

cook Maurice St. Clair   chief Reginald A. Doucette, Jr.

Tomato Spice Cake

The tomato flavor enhances the spices in this recipe, so the firehouse chef was right when he put the blush of tomato soup in this cake.

YIELDS FOUR 9″ LAYERS	INGREDIENTS	YIELDS TWO 9″ LAYERS
	Cake	
1 cup	Shortening	½ cup
2 cups	Sugar	1 cup
4	Eggs	2
4 cups	Flour	2 cups
4 tsp.	Baking powder	2 tsp.
½ tsp.	Salt	¼ tsp.
2 tsp.	Cinnamon	1 tsp.
1 tsp.	Cloves, ground	½ tsp.
2 tsp.	Nutmeg	1 tsp.
2 tsp.	Baking soda	1 tsp.
2 10¾-oz. cans	Tomato soup	1 10¾-oz. can
2 cups	Raisins	1 cup
2 cups	Walnuts or pecans, chopped	1 cup
	Frosting	
2 8-oz. pkg.	Cream cheese	8-ozs.
1½ to 2 1-lb. boxes	Powdered sugar	¾ to 1 1-lb. box
2 tsp.	Vanilla	1 tsp.

Blend shortening with the sugar. Beat in eggs. Sift together flour, baking powder, salt, cinnamon, cloves, and nutmeg. Dissolve baking soda in undiluted tomato soup. Mixture will bubble slightly.

Alternately add tomato soup and sifted dry ingredients to sugar-shortening-egg mixture. Stir in raisins and chopped nuts. Pour into greased and floured 9″ cake pans and bake in 350° oven until cake is brown and springs back when lightly touched. Allow cake to cool about ½ hour before removing to rack. Cream frosting ingredients together, adding powdered sugar gradually until frosting is the consistency you like. Spread evenly on cake.

Sparta-Style
Baked Lamb

Choosing a dish such as this hearty roast of three vegetables and a meat makes meal-planning at the Manchester firehouse simple yet rewarding.

SERVES 10	INGREDIENTS	SERVES 5
6½ to 7 lbs.	Leg of lamb	3½ to 4 lbs.
To taste	Salt and pepper	To taste
2	Garlic cloves	1
15 large	Baking potatoes	7 large
To taste	Oregano	To taste
8 cups	Green beans	4 cups
4	Onions	2
1 cup	White wine	½ cup

Rub the lamb with salt and pepper. Cut each clove of garlic into four slices. Make equally spaced gashes on fat side (under side) of lamb and insert pieces of garlic. Place lamb in roasting pan large enough for all ingredients. Peel and quarter potatoes and place around meat. Sprinkle lamb and potatoes with oregano to taste. Cover and bake at 325°, allowing 30 to 35 minutes per pound of meat. In a separate pan, cook beans for 15 minutes over medium heat. After lamb has cooked for half of total baking time, add green beans (drained), onions, and wine to pan. Return to oven, cover and continue baking until done, correcting seasoning before serving.

COOK Lou Ziakas   CHIEF John E. Davine

Brattleboro
Roast Beef

The reputation of this roast beef came about through invitations to outside guests, such as high school athletic teams and forest wardens, to fire department banquets.

SERVES 10	INGREDIENTS	SERVES 5
5 to 6 lbs.	Rump roast beef	3 to 4 lbs.
1 cup	Red wine	½ cup
1 cup	Corn oil	½ cup
½ tsp.	Celery salt	¼ tsp.
½ tsp.	Onion salt	¼ tsp.
½ tsp.	Seasoned salt	¼ tsp.
To taste	Salt and pepper	To taste
¼ cup (approx.)	Flour	2 Tbs. (approx.)

Combine wine, corn oil, and seasonings in bowl or measuring cup. Place roast in baking pan and baste with wine-oil mixture. Cover and roast in a 275° oven, basting every hour with pan juices until tender. Allow 35 minutes per pound for medium to well-done roast, 25 minutes for rare.

Gravy

Remove meat to warm platter and pour juices into a bowl. Skim fat from top, reserving several tablespoons for gravy. Just before serving brown the flour in the reserved fat in skillet on top of stove. Gradually add reserved liquid and allow the gravy to thicken, stirring constantly.

COOKS Howard T. Mattison and Lt. LeClaire
CHIEF Howard T. Mattison

Country-Style
Spareribs

Barbecued ribs are at home in any setting—on the firehouse table, in a comfortable farmhouse kitchen, or for a festive crowd.

SERVES 10	INGREDIENTS	SERVES 5
8 lbs.	Spareribs	4 lbs.
4 cups	Water	2 cups
1 cup	Onions	½ cup
2 cups	Catsup	1 cup
1 cups	Vinegar	½ cup
5 Tbs.	Sugar	2½ Tbs.
6 Tbs.	Worcestershire sauce	3 Tbs.
½ tsp.	Pepper	¼ tsp.
2 tsp.	Dry mustard	1 tsp.

Place spareribs in shallow baking pan with a rack on the bottom. Add water. Cover and bake at 300° for approximately 2 hours. While spareribs are cooking, chop the onions and combine with the rest of the ingredients in a saucepan. Bring to a boil, stirring well. Drain fat from spareribs and pour the hot sauce over them. Place ribs on middle rack under broiler and cook for about 20 minutes, turning once.

COOK Richard Trombley   CHIEF Patrick T. Brown

Pepper Burger

Firemen everywhere join the army of America is devoted to the hamburger. They may spice it with seasonings; serve it with onions, pickles, or tomatoes; add cheese, chili, or lettuce; grill it, pan-fry it, or bake it. It's an American food habit . . . it's a "burger." The recipe here uses Italian sausage and sweet roasted peppers.

YIELDS 12 PATTIES	INGREDIENTS	YIELDS 6 PATTIES
2 lbs.	Ground beef	1 lb.
2 large	Onions	1 large
1 lb.	Hot Italian sausage meat	½ lb.
8 Tbs.	Sweet roasted peppers	4 Tbs.
2	Garlic cloves, crushed	1
2	Eggs	1
To taste	MSG	To taste
1 tsp.	Kitchen Bouquet (or other brown gravy base)	½ tsp.
About 2 cups	Bread crumbs, plain or Italian	About 1 cup
To taste	Salt and pepper	To taste
6 to 8 Tbs.	Cooking oil	3 to 4 Tbs.
12	American cheese slices	6
12	Hamburger buns	6

Preheat the broiler. Chop the onions and sweet peppers. Combine ground beef, onions, and sausage meat. Add sweet roasted peppers, crushed garlic, eggs, MSG, and Kitchen Bouquet. (This last may be brushed on after patties are formed.) Add bread crumbs to obtain the right consistency for meat patties (about half of the amount specified), and salt and pepper to taste. Mix well and form into patties ¾-inch thick. Roll the patties in the remaining bread crumbs and fry slowly in cooking oil, turning until browned on both sides and cooked through. Remove to shallow baking pan. Top each patty with a cheese slice and place under broiler until cheese melts. Serve on hamburger buns with any additional garnish you like.

COOKS All personnel   CHIEF Merton E. Churchill

Chinese Chews

These Chinese Chews won't tell your fortune, but they will guarantee your popularity as a cook.

YIELDS TWO 8″ x 8″ PANS	INGREDIENTS	YIELDS ONE 8″ x 8″ PAN
	Cake	
2 cups	Flour	1 cup
4 Tbs.	Sugar	2 Tbs.
¼ tsp.	Salt	⅛ tsp.
1 cup	Margarine	½ cup
	Topping	
4 Tbs.	Flour	2 Tbs.
3 cups	Light brown sugar	1½ cups
4	Eggs	2
2 cups.	Walnuts or pecans, chopped	1 cup
2 tsp.	Vanilla	1 tsp.

Preheat oven to 375°. Sift flour for crust. Blend the flour, sugar, salt and margarine and pat the mixture into bottom of 8″ x 8″ pans, using the back of a teaspoon to spread evenly. Bake 10 to 15 minutes, or until browned. While crust is baking, mix ingredients for topping together in a bowl. Remove crust from oven and spread topping on baked crust. Return to oven, reduce heat to 350°, and bake approximately 15 minutes longer, or until brown on top. Cool and cut into small squares.

Variation: Coconut may be substituted for nuts, or both coconut and nuts may be used in topping.

Note: Oven temperatures can vary, therefore it is advisable to check for doneness fairly often during the short baking time.

COOK Hervey Dugas   CHIEF John F. McDonald

Stuffed Shells

This interesting pasta dish can be artfully prepared with a little practice. The shells should be carefully parbroiled for ease of handling while they are being stuffed with the cheese and egg mixture.

SERVES 12	INGREDIENTS	SERVES 6
28 to 32 (one 1-lb. box)	Jumbo macaroni shells	14 to 16 (half a 1-lb. box)
2 lbs.	Ricotta cheese	1 lb.
2	Eggs	1
To taste	Salt and pepper	To taste
½ lb.	Mozarella cheese, diced	¼ lb.
3 Tbs.	Romano or Parmesan cheese, grated	1½ Tbs.
2 15½-oz. jars	Spaghetti sauce	1 15½-oz. jar

Cook shells according to package directions for 9 or 10 minutes, or until half done. Rinse shells in cold water to stop cooking process and set them aside. In a bowl mix ricotta cheese, beaten eggs, salt, pepper, diced mozzarella, and grated cheese. Spread a thin layer of spaghetti sauce in the bottom of a large baking dish that has a tight-fitting cover. Using a teaspoon, fill each shell with about 2 tablespoons of the cheese-egg mixture. Place the filled shells in the baking dish in a single layer, and spoon the remaining sauce over them. Cover and bake in a 350° oven for 30 to 35 minutes.

COOK Robert Bradley   CHIEF Hans M. Lundgren

Bluefish
à la Shultz

"Shultz" is the nickname of the firefighter/fisherman who created this dish, which is his favorite way of preparing the fish he catches.

SERVES 12	INGREDIENTS	SERVES 6
12	Bluefish fillets	6
To taste	Salt and pepper	To taste
2	Lemons	1
6 Tbs.	Butter or margarine	3 Tbs.
1 tsp.	Oregano or parsley	½ tsp.
1 tsp.	Paprika	½ tsp.
	Parmesan cheese (optional)	

Making sure that all bones and skin have been removed from each fillet, divide into serving portions. Cut pieces of heavy aluminum foil into squares about 2″ larger than a single fillet. Place each fillet in the middle of a square of foil and roll the edges to form a kind of small pan. Season with salt and pepper. Cut fresh lemon into slices and place one on each fillet. (A few drops of concentrated lemon juice may be substituted.) Place a generous pat of butter or margarine on each piece of fish and sprinkle lightly with oregano or fresh parsley and paprika. Place the individual "pans" into a 400° oven and bake for about 20 minutes. For a crusty brown top, sprinkle a bit of Parmesan cheese on the fish after baking and run under the broiler for an additional 5 minutes.

COOK Bob Schluensen   CHIEF William H. Dawson

Crêpes Suzette

The chef here, a master of the art of preparing crêpes, advises, "A little practice will determine the proper consistency of the batter." His directions will help make your practice perfect.

YIELDS ABOUT 24	INGREDIENTS	YIELDS ABOUT 12
	Crêpes	
6	Eggs	3
2 cups	Flour	1 cup
½ tsp.	Vanilla	¼ tsp.
About 2 cups	Milk	About 1 cup
½ cup	Shortening	¼ cup

Filling

A choice of your favorite jellies, jams, pot cheese, blueberries, or strawberries and whipped cream

To sprinkle on crêpes	Powdered sugar or flaming brandy	To sprinkle on crêpes

Beat the eggs until light and frothy. Sift the flour, and slowly add it to the eggs, one tablespoon at a time, until consistency is that of a heavy pancake batter. Add vanilla. Gradually add the milk to the batter until the consistency is that of heavy cream. If too thick, add more milk; if too thin, add more flour. In a 6-inch or 8-inch frying pan heat the shortening. Two frying pans will prove useful; fry in one, keep the shortening heated in the other. In the second frying pan, used for cooking the crêpes, place one teaspoon of the melted shortening, roll the pan to just coat the bottom, and pour off any excess. Pour a few tablespoons of batter in pan, rolling the pan so the batter just covers the bottom to keep the crêpe as thin as possible. With small spatula or knife blade, lift edge of crêpe to check until it browns. Turn and brown other side. Place on heated platter. Choose your favorite filling and spread on crêpe. Roll into cylinder shape and sprinkle with powered sugar or flaming brandy.

COOK Bob Schluensen   CHIEF William H. Dawson

Firehouse
Blueberry Pancakes

SERVES 8	INGREDIENTS	SERVES 4
2 cups	Flour	1 cup
4 tsp.	Baking powder	2 tsp.
1 tsp.	Salt	½ tsp.
2 Tbs.	Sugar	1 Tbs.
2	Eggs	1
2 cups	Milk	1 cup
4 Tbs.	Butter, melted	2 Tbs.
1 cup	Blueberries, frozen or canned	½ cup

Sift together the flour, baking powder, salt, and sugar. Add the eggs and milk and beat all ingredients well. Stir in the melted butter. Drain and reserve juice from frozen or canned blueberries and stir the berries into batter. Heat a griddle and grease only slightly. Brown pancakes quickly on both sides, turning only once.
Serve with melted butter and your favorite syrup, jelly, or jam.

Suggestion: A fruit syrup can be made to serve over pancakes using reserved liquid from blueberries. Allow ½ cup blueberry juice to ¼ cup of sugar and cook in saucepan until thickened.

COOK Bob Schluensen   CHIEF William H. Dawson

Baked Stuffed
Flounder Fillets

SERVES 8	INGREDIENTS	SERVES 4
2 cups	Bread crumbs	1 cup
2	Eggs	1
¼ to ½ cup	Olive oil	⅛ to ¼ cup
To taste	Parsley	To taste
4 Tbs.	Onion, chopped (optional)	2 Tbs.
½ tsp.	Tarragon (optional)	¼ tsp.
1 lb.	Shrimp, diced	½ lb.
1 lb.	Scallops, diced	½ lb.
To taste	Salt and pepper	To taste
To taste	Garlic salt	To taste
½ cup	Water or dry white wine	¼ cup
16	Flounder fillets	8

Lemon and Butter Sauce

2	Lemons	1
½ lb.	Butter	¼ lb.
1 cup	Water	½ cup
2 Tbs.	Sugar	1 Tbs.
4 Tbs.	Parsley	2 Tbs.

Combine bread crumbs, eggs, olive oil, parsley, chopped onion, tarragon, shimp, and scallops in bowl. Add salt, pepper, and garlic salt to taste, and mix well. Add water or wine as needed to make a proper consistency for stuffing. Put stuffing in large end of fillet and roll up. Make a single layer of the rolls, seam down, in a baking dish.

Sauce: Cut lemons in half, squeeze juice into saucepan, and place lemon halves in pan with juice. Add butter, water, sugar, and parsley. Heat until butter has melted. Pour sauce over stuffed fillets. Bake in 375° oven 30 minutes, basting fillets once or twice with sauce during this time.

cook Donald R. Hennessey   chief Francis J. Sweeney

Baked Stuffed
Pork Chops

The Assistant Chief who prepares this recipe says it has been given a four-star rating in Yonkers. He bakes apples along with the chops and adds, "as long as the oven is going, you may just as well bake a few potatoes!"

SERVES 12	INGREDIENTS	SERVES 6
12	Pork chops, thick center cut	6
2 Tbs.	Cooking oil	1 Tbs.
12 slices	White bread	6 slices
½ cup	Celery	¼ cup
½ lb.	Fresh pork sausage meat	¼ lb.
1 medium	Onion	1 small
½ cup	Margarine	¼ cup
To taste	Poultry seasoning	To taste
To taste	Thyme (optional)	To taste
To taste	Salt and pepper	To taste
About 2 cups	Milk	About 1 cup

Cut a pocket in each pork chop for stuffing. Brown the chops in a skillet in the cooking oil, and set them aside. Dice the bread and finely chop the celery and onion. Place sausage in skillet and sauté slowly, draining off excess fat. Add the onion and celery to the sausage and cook over low heat for about 5 minutes. Add diced bread, margarine, and seasonings to the skillet only long enough to melt margarine. Remove from heat and mix the ingredients thoroughly. Stuff pork chops with bread and sausage mixture, and put the chops in a baking dish. Pour enough milk over the chops to cover them by ¼". Salt and pepper lightly. Cover baking dish

securely with aluminum foil and bake for 60 to 70 minutes in a 350°
oven.

Suggestion: Serve with baked apples (see following recipe), baked
potatoes with butter or sour cream, and a favorite seasonal
vegetable.

Baked Apples

SERVES 12	INGREDIENTS	SERVES 6
12	Baking apples	6
About ½ cup	Raisins	About ¼ cup
½ cup	Dark brown sugar	¼ cup
12 tsp.	Water	6 tsp.
½ cup	Light corn syrup	¼ cup
½ cup	Margarine	¼ cup
	Cinnamon	

Core the apples and set them in a lightly greased baking dish. Half-fill each center with raisins and fill to the top with brown sugar. Pour a teaspoon of water into each, then drizzle a teaspoon of corn syrup over apple. Place a small square of margarine in the core and sprinkle the tops with cinnamon. Bake in 350° oven for 30 to 40 minutes. Serve warm.

COOK Edward T. Dunn   CHIEF Andrew J. Gerlock

Pickled Beets

This recipe was received with a menu-planning hint from the firehouse chef to serve it "with all the recipes for chops and steaks you'll have in your book."

YIELDS ABOUT ONE QUART	INGREDIENTS	YIELDS ABOUT ONE PINT
1½ cups	Cider vinegar	¾ cup
⅓ cup	Sugar	About 2½ Tbs.
½ tsp.	Salt	¼ tsp.
¼ tsp.	Pepper	⅛ tsp.
2	Bay leaves	1
5 whole	Cloves	2 whole
2 16-oz. cans or 3 lbs. fresh	Cooked beets	1 16-oz. can or 1½ lbs. fresh
	Onion slices (optional)	

Canned beets: Heat vinegar and sugar together. Add the seasonings and pour over cooked beets that have been drained and sliced. Add enough reserved liquid from the can to cover the beets. Add onion slices, if you choose. Chill until serving time.

Fresh beets: Choose beets of uniform size. Cut off the tops, leaving about 1″ of stem. Wash thoroughly, but do not scrub or break skin of beets. Cover with boiling water and simmer slowly, in covered pan, from 30 minutes to 1 hour (depending on size of beets) until beets are tender. Drain. Reserve liquid. Remove skins and stems when beets are cool enough to handle. Slice them and add to heated vinegar mixture. Heat just to simmering, adding reserved liquid if needed to cover beets. Add onions (if used) and serve chilled.

COOK Robert E. Curtin   CHIEF Alexander W. Leggat

Night-Watch Snack

A fireman in your vicinity—no matter where you live—is on duty every hour of every night, waiting for an emergency call. And while he waits, he may decide to cook himself a hamburger, open-face style.

SERVES 8	INGREDIENTS	SERVES 4
1 head	Lettuce	½ head
4	Tomatoes	2
2 lbs.	Ground beef	1 lb.
To taste	Salt and pepper	To taste
8	Sesame-seed hamburger rolls	4
16	Cheddar cheese slices	8
To taste	Mayonnaise	To taste

Chop lettuce, slice tomatoes, and place in refrigerator to chill until ready to use. Season and divide the ground beef into patties. Cook hamburgers. Just before they are ready, place the rolls, with a cheese slice on each half, under the broiler until the cheese melts. Remove the rolls and put the lettuce, tomato slices, and mayonnaise on the top half of each roll and a hamburger on each of the bottom halves. Serve open.

Suggestion: A choice of extra seasonings, such as garlic or onion salt, may be used when preparing beef patties.

COOK James Mooney   CHIEF Earl McCormick

Sausage and Sauce

This time-tested recipe is a favorite in Pittsburgh, where chef Anthony Caiaccia has been preparing it at No. 32 Engine Company for more than 15 years.

SERVES 8	INGREDIENTS	SERVES 4
4 lbs.	Hot Italian sausage	2 lbs.
2 1-lb., 13-oz. cans	Tomato purée	1 1-lb., 13-oz. can
2 tomato purée cans	Water	1 tomato purée can
2 12-oz. cans	Tomato paste	1 12-oz. can
2 tomato paste cans	Water	1 tomato paste can
4	Green peppers	2
8 small	Onions	4 small
1 tsp.	Salt	½ tsp.
1 tsp.	Garlic salt	½ tsp.
1 heaping Tbs.	Sugar	2 tsp.
1 heaping Tbs.	Italian seasoning	2 tsp.

Italian bread or buns

Brown the sausage links in a frying pan. In a large pot, heat the tomato purée and tomato paste with equal amounts of water for each can used. Cut the green peppers into ¼″ strips and add to the tomato sauce. Cut onions into half-rings and add to the sauce, along with the seasonings. Add the browned sausage and simmer for about 1½ hours. Fork the sausages onto Italian bread or buns, and cover with sauce. Refrigerate any remaining sauce for another meal. Add browned ground beef to heated left-over sauce. Pour over cooked spaghetti and sprinkle with Parmesan cheese. Serve with a tossed green salad.

COOK Anthony Caiaccia

FIREHOUSE RECIPES

from the
South Atlantic States

Pot Roast
with Spaghetti Sauce

At the No. 1 Station in Wilmington, firefighters contribute to a meal fund—one dollar for each man per meal, from soup to steak. Below is a menu favorite from the firehouse chef who plans the meals and does the cooking, with two men assigned to kitchen patrol.

SERVES 12	INGREDIENTS	SERVES 6
4 to 6 Tbs.	Shortening	3 to 4 Tbs.
6 lbs.	Beef pot roast	3 lbs.
2 1-lb., 12-oz. cans	Tomato purée	1 1-lb., 12-oz. can
3 12-oz. cans	Tomato paste	3 6-oz. cans
1 can for each can of purée and paste, plus one additional large can	Water	1 can for each can of purée and paste, plus one additional large can
3 tsp.	Rosemary	1½ tsp.
3 tsp.	Oregano	1½ tsp.
To taste	Garlic salt	To taste
To taste	Salt	To taste
3 tsp.	Basil	1½ tsp.
3 Tbs.	Onions, minced	1½ Tbs.
2 tsp.	Hot red-pepper sauce	1 tsp.
2	Bay leaf	1

Heat the shortening in a frying pan and brown the roast well on all sides. Combine tomato purée and paste in a deep, heavy pot and add water. Add all seasoning, and heat until the sauce boils. Reduce heat and add the browned pot roast. Cook over low heat uncovered for approximately 3 hours. Chop meat and serve in sauce over spaghetti, or serve meat separately with sauce and spaghetti as an accompaniment.

Note: Other cuts of meat (stew beef, round steak, or meatballs) may be used in this sauce instead of pot roast.

Garlic Bread

According to the chef at No. 1 Station in Wilmington, the job isn't bad at all. In the completely modern firehouse kitchen, with all new appliances, it's "just a matter of getting it all together."

SERVES 12	INGREDIENTS	SERVES 4
4 loaves	French bread	1 loaf
To taste	Garlic salt	To taste
About 1 cup	Butter	About ¼ cup
2 tsp.	Oregano	½ tsp.
¼ cup	Onions, minced	2 Tbs.

Slice bread almost all the way through in ¾″ slices. Between each slice sprinkle garlic salt lightly. Insert a generous pat of butter between each slice, and spread softened butter over the top crust of each loaf. Sprinkle a little oregano and minced onions over each loaf. Wrap in foil, leaving top open. Heat in a 250° oven for 10 to 15 minutes, or until all butter is melted.

COOK Anthony V. Santucci   CHIEF John J. Malloy

Fish or
Crab Cakes

SERVES 10	INGREDIENTS	SERVES 5
2 lbs.	Fish or crab	1 lb.
2	Eggs	1
2 heaping Tbs.	Mayonnaise	1 heaping Tbs.
2 tsp.	Mustard (dry)	1 tsp.
2 Tbs.	Seafood seasoning	1 Tbs.
To taste	Salt and pepper	To taste
About 2 cups	Bread or cracker crumbs	About 1 cup
For deep frying	Cooking oil	For deep frying

Bone the fish and mash well. Combine all ingredients and shape into cakes. Cook in deep fryer at 365° to 385° until golden brown.

COOK Francis C. Fantom   CHIEF J. Austin Deitz

Tomato Aspic

YIELDS TWO RING MOLDS TO SERVE 12	INGREDIENTS	YIELDS ONE RING MOLD TO SERVE 6
3⅓ cups	Tomato juice	1⅔ cups
2 tsp.	Onion juice	1 tsp.
3 Tbs.	Vinegar	1¼ Tbs.
¼ tsp.	Paprika	⅛ tsp.
½ tsp.	Celery salt	¼ tsp.
¼ tsp.	Cloves, ground	⅛ tsp.
2 3-oz. pkgs.	Lemon gelatin	1 3-oz. pkg.

Combine the tomato juice, onion juice, and vinegar in a saucepan with the seasonings. Bring to a boil, and pour into a bowl over the gelatin. Stir to dissolve. When cool, pour into ring molds and refrigerate until set. Serve on lettuce leaves with mayonnaise dressing.

COOK Fire Department Auxiliary   CHIEF Frank S. Tremel

Buttermilk Pound Cake

YIELDS TWO TUBE PANS	INGREDIENTS	YIELDS ONE TUBE PAN
1 cup	Butter	½ cup
1 cup	Shortening or margarine	½ cup
4 cups	Sugar	2 cups
8	Eggs	4
5½ cups	Flour	2¾ cups
1 tsp.	Baking powder	½ tsp.
1 tsp.	Baking soda	½ tsp.
1 tsp.	Salt	½ tsp.
2 cups	Buttermilk	1 cup
2 tsp.	Vanilla	1 tsp.
2 tsp.	Lemon or almond extract	1 tsp.

Preheat oven to 325°. Cream butter and shortening or margarine with sugar. Add eggs and beat well. Sift together the flour, baking powder, baking soda, and salt. Add the dry ingredients gradually to the butter-sugar mixture, alternating with the buttermilk, and beating after each addition. Add flavoring and beat again. Bake in greased, lightly floured tube pan for 45 minutes to 1 hour, or until a toothpick comes out clean.

COOK Fire Department Auxiliary   CHIEF Frank S. Tremel

Apple-Oatmeal Squares

YIELDS TWO 8″ x 8″ PANS	INGREDIENTS	YIELDS ONE 8″ x 8″ PAN
1 cup	Butter or margarine	½ cup
2 cups	Flour	1 cup
1½ cups	3-minute oatmeal	¾ cup
1 cup	Brown sugar	½ cup
1 cup	White sugar	½ cup
1 tsp.	Baking soda	½ tsp.
1 tsp.	Cinnamon	½ tsp.
4	Apples	2
½ tsp.	Additional cinnamon	¼ tsp.

Melt butter in a small saucepan over low heat, and set aside. Mix the next six dry ingredients together. Generously butter or grease pans. Spread half of dry mixture evenly over bottom of pans. Slice peeled apples thinly and place slices in even layers on top of dry mixture. Drizzle ⅓ of melted butter over apples, top with the remaining dry ingredients, and pour remaining butter over the mixture. Sprinkle lightly with additional cinnamon. Bake in a 350° oven for 40 to 45 minutes, or until brown. Cool and cut into squares.

COOK Fire Department Auxiliary   CHIEF Frank S. Tremel

Beef Chow Mein

SERVES 10	INGREDIENTS	SERVES 5
3 lbs.	Round steak	1½ lbs.
3 Tbs.	Cooking oil	1½ Tbs.
3 cups	Onions, chopped coarsely	1½ cups
3 cups	Water	1½ cups
2	Bouillon cubes	1
1 cup	Green peppers, chopped	½ cup
3 Tbs.	Soy sauce	1½ Tbs.
2 Tbs.	Brown sugar	1 Tbs.
2 No. 2 can	Bean sprouts	1 No. 2 can
6 Tbs.	Cornstarch	3 Tbs.
½ cup	Water	¼ cup
To taste	Salt and pepper	To taste

Rice or chow-mein noodles

Trim the steak and cut it into bite-size pieces. Fry the meat quickly in oil over high heat until it is browned. Then add the onions and continue cooking until onions are almost done, about 5 minutes. Dissolve the bouillon cubes in hot water. Add the green peppers, soy sauce, bouillon, brown sugar, and bean sprouts to the meat and onions. Bring to boiling point and stir in the cornstarch, already dissolved in a few tablespoons of water. Salt and pepper to taste and cook, uncovered, over medium heat, stirring occasionally until mixture thickens. Serve over rice or chow-mein noodles.

cook Eldridge Brown   chief David B. Gratz

Firehouse Apple Pie

Any dish as American as apple pie just has to be popular in firehouses all over America. Here at the Silver Spring fire department, it's a special favorite.

YIELDS TWO 9″ PIES	INGREDIENTS	YIELDS ONE 9″ PIE
16	Cooking apples	8
1½ cups	Sugar	¾ cup
2 tsp.	Cinnamon	1 tsp.
½ tsp.	Salt	¼ tsp.
2 Tbs.	Cornstarch	1 Tbs.
½ cup	Butter	¼ cup
For two double-crust pies	Pastry mix or basic recipe	For one double-crust pie
3 Tbs.	Milk	1½ Tbs.

Prepare the pastry, using a pie-crust mix or basic recipe. Peel, core, and thinly slice the apple and layer the slices in the unbaked bottom pie shell. Mix sugar, cinnamon, salt, and cornstarch together in small bowl and sprinkle over the apples. Dot with butter and place the top crust over the apples. Seal the edges together and brush the top with milk. Bake at 350° for 40 to 50 minutes, until crust is golden brown.

COOK Eldridge Brown   CHIEF David B. Gratz

Frozen Vanilla Custard

This recipe mixture is frozen in an old two-gallon hand-cranked freezer. Eldridge Brown, who prepares the dish, also furnishes the ice-cream maker, a 1923 model purchased 25 years ago at auction for 25 cents.

YIELDS TWO GALLONS	INGREDIENTS	YIELDS ONE GALLON
6 13-oz. cans	Evaporated milk	3 13-oz. cans
5 cups	Water	2½ cups
6	Eggs	3
3½ cups	Sugar	1¾ cups
3 Tbs.	Cornstarch	1½ Tbs.
½ tsp.	Salt	¼ tsp.
2 Tbs. plus 1 tsp.	Vanilla	1 Tbs. plus 1 tsp.
	Crushed ice	
	Rock salt	

Combine half of the evaporated milk with all the water in a large pan. Add the lightly beaten eggs. Mix the sugar with the cornstarch and salt in separate bowl, and add to the milk-egg mixture. Cook and stir over low heat until sugar is dissolved and mixture is thick enough to coat a spoon, about 15 to 20 minutes. Add the remaining milk and the vanilla. Pack crushed ice and rock salt in the freezer according to the directions on the rock salt container. Turn until mixture becomes frozen.

Suggestion: Sweet milk may be substituted for water for a richer ice cream.

COOK Eldridge Brown   CHIEF David B. Gratz

Clam Chowder

The cooks in firehouse kitchens have a simple aim: to prepare wholesome food which tastes good. Two meals a day are served at the Norfolk stations, with all men sharing the expenses.

SERVES 16	INGREDIENTS	SERVES 8
2 doz.	Clams, large fresh	1 doz.
2 qts.	Water	1 qt.
4 cups	Onions, chopped	2 cups
1 stalk	Celery, chopped	½ stalk
1 tsp.	Thyme	½ tsp.
1 tsp.	MSG	½ tsp.
6	Carrots, diced	3
1 lb.	Salt pork	½ lb.
8 cups	Potatoes, diced	4 cups
To taste	Salt and pepper	To taste

Wash the clams and put them in about ½" of water in a large kettle. Cover the kettle and steam until all the clams have opened their shells, about 5 to 10 minutes. Discard any that are still shut. Remove the clams from the kettle, reserving the broth, and cool. Shell the clams and cut into pieces. Add the onions, celery, thyme, MSG, and carrots to the broth. Simmer for 45 minutes, covered. Dice the salt pork and fry in a skillet until crisp. Drain on paper towel and add to the broth. Add clams, potatoes, salt, and pepper, and more water, if desired. Cover and cook until all ingredients are done, about 8 to 10 minutes.

COOK James R. Taylor   CHIEF Bert Wilson

Strawberries in the Snow

The chef here says that although the men rib him about his cooking, he notices that seldom is anything thrown away. Despite the kidding, he enjoys cooking, and the hardest part of the job is deciding what to have in the first place.

SERVES 16	INGREDIENTS	SERVES 8
1 large	Angel-food cake	½ large or 1 small
8 ozs.	Cream cheese	4 ozs.
1 cup	Sugar	½ cup
4 cups	Whipped cream or whipped-cream substitute	2 cups
2 pkgs. frozen or 1 qt. fresh, sliced and sugared	Strawberries	1 pkg. frozen or 1 pt. fresh, sliced and sugared

Cut the cake into 1″ slices and cover the bottom of a shallow pan with them. Soften the cream cheese and combine with the sugar. Beat the whipped cream with the cream cheese and sugar mixture with a rotary or electric mixer until the mixture forms stiff peaks. Pour some of the strawberry juice onto the cake, and cover the cake with the whipped topping. Spread the strawberries over the topping, letting some of the juice penetrate the topping. Chill and serve.

COOK Robert E. Anderson   CHIEF W. C. Bray

Macaroni-Sausage
Casserole

The firemen in Newport News all agree that this is a favorite recipe at Station 3. For a hurry-up supper, baking time may be omitted and the cooking done entirely on top of the stove. For a tasty and economical meal, serve this casserole with cole slaw and applesauce.

SERVES 10 TO 12	INGREDIENTS	SERVES 5 TO 6
1 lb.	Macaroni	½ lb.
2 lbs.	Pork sausage meat	1 lb.
2 large	Onions	1 large
4 to 6 stalks	Celery	2 to 3 stalks
2 No. 2½ cans	Tomatoes	1 No. 2½ can
To taste	Salt and pepper	To taste
1 lb.	Sharp cheddar cheese, grated	½ lb.

Cook the macaroni according to package directions and drain. Brown the sausage in a skillet while you chop the onions and celery. After about five minutes' cooking time, add them to the sausage. When sausage is done, tilt the pan and remove the excess grease with a spoon. Add the chopped tomatoes (with juice from can), salt, and pepper, and simmer for 5 to 10 minutes. Combine the macaroni and the sausage mixture in a shallow casserole dish. Sprinkle grated cheese on top and bake in 400° oven for 15 to 20 minutes, or until cheese is melted.

COOK L. T. Crafford   CHIEF C. L. Kegley

Braised Beef with Noodles

An easy-to-prepare and flavorful dish can be created by baking braised beef in vegetable juice with onions. It's delicious as meat-and-sauce served over noodles or as a meat entree along with fresh vegetables or a fruit salad.

SERVES 12	INGREDIENTS	SERVES 4
6 lbs.	Chuck beef, cut in 1½″ cubes	2 lbs.
2 cups	Flour	⅔ cup
1 Tbs.	Salt	1 tsp.
1 tsp.	Pepper	¼ tsp.
¾ tsp.	Paprika	¼ tsp.
¼ to ½ cup	Cooking oil	⅛ to ¼ cup
4 medium	Onions	1 large
4 cups	Vegetable juice	2 cups
1 tsp.	Worcestershire sauce	Dash or two
1 No. 303 can	Green peas	⅔ cup
To taste	Additional salt and pepper	To taste
	Noodles	
4 Tbs.	Butter	2 Tbs.
⅔ cup	Cheddar cheese, grated (optional)	⅓ cup

Roll meat in flour that has been seasoned with salt, pepper, and paprika. Brown beef in heated cooking oil in frying pan, using only enough oil to keep meat from sticking to pan. Place meat in roasting pan. Cut onions into eighths. Add to meat. Add V-8 juice, Worcestershire, salt and pepper to taste. Cover. Bake in moderate oven (350°) for 1 hour or until meat is tender. Add peas during last 10 minutes of cooking time. Serve over cooked, buttered noodles. Sprinkle with grated cheese, if desired.

COOKS All personnel CHIEF John F. Finnegan, Jr.

Har-Grot Potatoes

The unusual title of this recipe comes from the name of the chef who invented this unique way of preparing an old favorite.

SERVES 12 TO 14	INGREDIENTS	SERVES 4 TO 6
10	Potatoes	3
3	Onions	1
3 cans	Cheese sauce	1 can
1 cup	Water	⅓ cup
1 13-oz. can	Evaporated milk	4 ozs.
1tsp.	Salt	⅓ tsp.
1 tsp.	Pepper	⅓ tsp.
3 Tbs.	Parmesan cheese	1 Tbs.

Peel the potatoes and onions and cut both into ¼-inch slices. Separate the onions into rings. Alternate layers of potato slices and onion rings in a greased baking dish. In a bowl combine the cheese sauce, water, milk, salt, and pepper, and pour over potatoes and onions. Sprinkle the top with Parmesan cheese and bake in 375° oven for approximately 55 minutes, or until potatoes are tender when tested with a fork.

COOK M. L. Harman   CHIEF John F. Finnegan, Jr.

Venison Steak

SERVES 8	INGREDIENTS	SERVES 4
8 pieces (4 lbs.)	Venison steak	4 pieces (2 lbs.)
As needed	Water	As needed
2 tsp.	Baking soda	1 tsp.
2 Tbs.	Vinegar	1 Tbs.
2 cups	Flour	1 cup
1 tsp.	Salt	½ tsp.
½ tsp.	Pepper	¼ tsp.
½ cup	Shortening	¼ cup
1 medium	Onion, sliced	1 small
2 stalks	Celery, chopped	1 stalk
2 cups	Water	1 cup

Cover steak with a mixture of hot water, baking soda, and vinegar. Let stand for 5 minutes. Rinse the pieces of steak well in cold water and dry with a paper towel. Season with salt and pepper and roll in the flour. Heat the shortening in a frying pan and brown the meat quickly on both sides. Place the browned steaks in a roasting pan and cover with the sliced onions and celery. Add water and bake, covered, in a 375° oven until tender (approximately 1 hour and 40 minutes).

COOK Morris F. Bailey   CHIEF Claud L. Nelson

Breaded
Pork Chops

SERVES 12	INGREDIENTS	SERVES 6
12	Pork chops, center cut	6
2	Eggs	1
2½ cups	Milk	1¼ cups
2 Tbs.	Worcestershire sauce	1 Tbs.
3 cups	Cracker meal	1½ cups
½ tsp.	Poultry seasoning	¼ tsp.
½ tsp.	Sage	¼ tsp.
½ tsp.	Celery seed	¼ tsp.
½ tsp.	Garlic salt	¼ tsp.
6 to 8 Tbs.	Cooking oil	2 to 4 Tbs.

Pound the pork chops on both sides with meat hammer to tenderize. Mix together the eggs, milk, and Worcestershire sauce. In a separate bowl make a dry mixture using the cracker meal, poultry seasoning, sage, celery seed, and garlic salt. Dip the chops first into the egg-milk mixture and then into the cracker meal, coating both sides. Fry the chops in heated cooking oil in a skillet until browned, about 10 minutes. Remove the chops to a baking dish, placing them on a rack so that the baked-out excess grease may be caught below the meat. Bake, uncovered, in a 350° oven until chops are slightly crusty, about 30 minutes.

cook Harold G. Enoch   chief C. Dale Pringle

Potato Dish from Truck Co. No. 2

*The men at Central Station divide the cooking duties by
assigning the job to a different company each week—one man
cooks and three others wash the pots and pans. The men say
they can tell from the menu which shift is doing the cooking.
Here is one of their best recipes—a crispy, cheese-topped
potato dish that is very easy to prepare.*

SERVES 10	INGREDIENTS	SERVES 5
5 lbs.	Baking potatoes	2½ lbs.
½ lb.	Margarine	¼ lb.
4 slices	White bread	2 slices
½ lb.	Sharp cheddar cheese	¼ lb.
To taste	Salt	To taste

Peel and cut the potatoes into ¼ " slices. Melt the margarine and
dip in potatoes, one by one. Arrange the potatoes in a flat baking
pan no more than 2 slices deep. Toast the bread and crumble or
grate the slices over the potatoes. Drizzle any remaining margarine
over the potatoes. Grate the cheese and sprinkle over the dish.
Cook in 350° oven for 25 minutes, or until potatoes have a crisp,
brown topping. Salt to taste.

Note: The original firehouse recipe had an ingredients listing cal-
culated to serve 20. We cut it down to 10 to conform with most of
our other recipes. However, if you'd like to have a "potato race"
with the men in Greensboro, just double the larger serving amount.

COOKS All personnel   CHIEF G. C. Wuchae

Carolina
Coconut Pie

YIELDS TWO 9″ PIES	INGREDIENTS	YIELDS ONE 9″ PIE
	Filling	
1½ cups	Sugar	¾ cup
⅔ cup	Flour	⅓ cup
½ tsp.	Salt	¼ tsp.
4 cups	Milk	2 cups
6	Egg yolks	3
4 tsp.	Butter	2 tsp.
2 tsp.	Vanilla	1 tsp.
2 cups	Coconut	1 cup
	Meringue	
6	Egg whites	3
¼ tsp.	Salt	⅛ tsp.
12 Tbs.	Sugar	6 Tbs.
2 9″ shells	Pie pastry, baked	1 9″ shell

Filling: Combine the sugar, flour, and salt in a saucepan, blending very well so that the flour will not become lumpy when heated. Gradually add the milk and cook over medium heat. Bring to a boil, stirring constantly to prevent sticking. Continue to cook and stir for several minutes, until consistency is that of mayonnaise. Remove from heat. Stir a small amount of this custard into the egg yolks until the yolks are heated through. Stir the egg-yolk mixture into the custard and add butter, vanilla, and coconut, reserving enough coconut to sprinkle on top of pie. Pour the filling into the baked pie shells and allow to cool while you make the meringue.

Meringue: Beat the egg whites with salt until they form stiff peaks. Gradually add the sugar and continue beating until meringue is is thick and glossy. Spread evenly over the custard filling. Sprinkle with reserved coconut and run under the broiler for a golden-brown surface.

Catfish Stew

The procedure for preparing a perfect fish chowder was given to us by Columbia Fire Captain R. O. Hoover. Although the Captain prefers catfish, almost any kind of boned fish can be substituted with satisfying results.

SERVES 10	INGREDIENTS	SERVES 5
3 lbs.	Onions	1½ lbs.
½ cup	Margarine	¼ cup
1 lb.	Salted bacon or fatback	½ lb.
5 lbs.	Catfish, cleaned	2½ lbs.
4 qts.	Water	2 qts.
3 lbs.	Potatoes	1½ lbs.
3 10¾-oz. cans	Tomato soup	1½ 10¾-oz cans
To taste	Salt and pepper	To taste
1 5¼-oz. can	Evaporated milk (optional)	2 to 3 ozs.

Dice the onions. Melt the margarine in a skillet, and cook the onions over medium-high heat for about 3 minutes; lower the flame and sauté gently for another 15 minutes. Remove from heat and set aside. Dice the bacon by cross-cutting in ½" squares, discarding skin. Fry the bacon pieces until crisp in a separate skillet. Remove bacon from pan, reserving bacon fat. Place fish in a large pot, cover with hot water and simmer, covered, until done, or about 20 minutes. Remove fish from water, bone and flake, and return to water. Add reserved onions and bacon fat. (Add bacon, if desired.) Simmer 10 to 15 additional minutes. Peel and dice the potatoes and add them along with the tomato soup to the fish. Season to taste with salt and pepper and simmer until potatoes are done, about 15 to 20 minutes. Stir often while stew is cooking. For additional richness, add a small amount of evaporated milk.

COOK R. O. Hoover   CHIEF H. Bert Dickert

Fruit Salad
with Sour Cream

When Chief Guthre received our request for a recipe, he chose W. E. Alverson as the chef for the job. Firefighter Alverson graciously obliged us with this recipe.

SERVES 8 TO 10	INGREDIENTS	SERVES 4 TO 6
1 No. 303 can	Fruit cocktail	1 cup
1 No. 2 can	Pineapple chunks	1 No. 1 can
1 No. 303 can	Sliced peaches	1 cup
6 ozs.	Coconut	3 ozs.
1 cup	Walnut pieces	½ cup
2 1½-oz. boxes	Raisins	1 1½-oz. box
2	Bananas, sliced	1
1 pt.	Sour cream	1 cup

Drain the canned fruit. Combine all fruits and nuts and stir in sour cream. Chill for 2 hours before serving.

COOK W. E. Alverson   CHIEF W. E. Guthre

Swiss Steak

*This popular steak dish can be baked in the oven or simmered
on top of the stove, whichever you choose.*

SERVES 8 TO 10	INGREDIENTS	SERVES 4 TO 6
4 lbs.	Round steak	2 lbs.
⅔ cup	Flour	⅓ cup
To taste	Salt and pepper	To taste
6 Tbs.	Shortening	3 Tbs.
1	Green pepper	½
2	Onions	1
3 No. 2 cans	Tomatoes	1 No. 2½ can

Dredge the steak in flour seasoned with salt and pepper. Melt the
shortening in a frying pan, and brown the meat quickly on both
sides. Remove the steak from the pan and place in a roasting pan.
Chop the green pepper, onion, and tomatoes and pour with tomato
juice from can over steak. Bake 1 hour at 300° to 350° with a
tight lid on the roasting pan. (You may simmer this dish on top
of the stove in the same pan used to brown the meat. Cover tightly
and simmer on low heat for 1 to 1½ hours.)

COOK W. E. Alverson   CHIEF W. E. Guthre

Crash Cake

This is a quick way to prepare a different and delicious pudding cake. It is mixed in the same pan it is baked and served in.

YIELDS TWO TUBE PANS	INGREDIENTS	YIELDS ONE TUBE PAN
2 No. 2 cans	Crushed pineapple	1 No. 2 can
2 No. 2 cans	Cherry-pie filling	1 No. 2 can
2 boxes	Yellow cake mix	1 box
1 cup	Pecans	½ cup
½ lb.	Butter or margarine	¼ lb.

Pour the pineapple with its juice and the cherry-pie filling into the bottom of a tube pan. Stir briefly. Sprinkle the cake mix over the fruit and stir again until the dry mix is thoroughly moist. Sprinkle nuts over the mixture and pour melted butter over the top. Bake at 300° for approximately 1 hour. The finished cake should have a pudding consistency. Serve it by spooning from the pan.

COOK W. E. Alverson   CHIEF W. E. Guthre

Fried Liver
and Bulldog Gravy

If you're a liver-lover you'll be pleased with the very special recipe given here. If you're not a liver-lover, I guess no recipe will help you—not even this one.

SERVES 10	INGREDIENTS	SERVES 5
5 lbs.	Beef or calf's liver, sliced medium thin	2½ lbs.
To taste	Salt and pepper	To taste
2 cups	Flour	1 cup
1 lb.	Margarine	½ lb.
2 small cans	Evaporated milk	1 small can
10 cups	Water	5 cups

Wash and dry the liver; salt and pepper to taste. Dip each portion in flour and sauté in margarine over medium heat until browned on both sides. Remove to a heated serving platter.

Bulldog Gravy

Add salt and pepper to the drippings in the skillet. Add enough flour to the pan to make a gravy (1 tablespoon for each tablespoon of fat) and cook the flour and fat mixture, stirring, until browned. Add milk and water to the pan until desired consistency is obtained.

Note: If desired, onions may be added to the gravy and slowly simmered until done.

COOK L. C. Garrett   CHIEF J. E. Poole

Banana Pudding

An all-time dessert favorite of everyone is banana pudding. Dave Porter, the chef at the Greenville firehouse, has the right combination of ingredients for a delicious pudding.

SERVES 12	INGREDIENTS	SERVES 6
	Pudding	
1⅓ cup	Sugar	⅔ cup
4 Tbs.	Flour	2 Tbs.
4 cups	Whole milk or equal parts evaporated milk and water	2 cups
4	Egg yolks	2
2 heaping Tbs.	Butter	1 heaping Tbs.
2 tsp.	Vanilla	1 tsp.
About 50	Vanilla wafers	About 25
6 or 7	Bananas	4 or 5
	Meringue	
4	Egg whites	2
⅛ tsp.	Salt	a pinch
4 Tbs.	Sugar	2 Tbs.
¼ tsp.	Vanilla (optional)	⅛ tsp.

Mix the sugar and flour thoroughly in a saucepan. Add milk and stir well; mix in the beaten egg yolks. Add butter and bring the mixture to a boil over medium heat, stirring constantly to blend all ingredients and prevent sticking. Remove from heat immediately after boiling point is reached and add vanilla. Cool. In a baking dish arrange a layer of vanilla wafers, then a layer of bananas, and pour a few spoonfuls of filling over the layers. Continue to add layers of wafers, bananas and filling until all of the filling is used.

Make the meringue icing by beating the egg whites until stiff. Add salt, and a little vanilla for flavoring, if desired, and stir well. Spread on pudding and broil until the top is lightly browned. This won't take very long, so keep a sharp eye on the broiler.

COOK Dave Porter   CHIEF J. E. Poole

Chef's Salad

This salad is a firehouse favorite in Atlanta in the summertime.
It is served with soda crackers and a cold drink and contains
"everything but the kitchen sink."

SERVES 12	INGREDIENTS	SERVES 6
4 oz.	Elbow macaroni	2 oz.
6	Hard-boiled eggs	3
2 7-oz. cans	Tuna fish	1 7-oz. can
3 or 4	Tomatoes	2
1 cup	Cheddar cheese	½ cup
1 cup	Sweet pickles	½ cup
4 or 5 slices	Bologna	2 slices
4 or 5 slices	Salami	2 slices
1 medium	Onion	1 small
6	Radishes	3
½ cup or more	Mayonnaise	¼ cup or more
To taste	Salt and pepper	To taste
2 heads	Lettuce	1 head

Cook the macaroni according to package directions and drain. Meanwhile chop and dice the eggs, fish, vegetables, cheese, and meat. Combine them with the cooked macaroni and add enough mayonnaise to bind. Salt and pepper to taste. Toss and serve on washed and dried lettuce leaves.

COOK J. R. Pittman   CHIEF P. O. Williams

Congealed Salad

The Battalion Chief, dubbed "No. 1 Chef" in charge of special functions at Atlanta's fire department, rates this salad a favorite and on one occasion 450 servings were made from this recipe. It is often served at the firehouse as a summertime side-dish with cold turkey or chicken.

SERVES 16 TO 18	INGREDIENTS	SERVES 8 TO 10
2 8-oz. cans	Crushed pineapple	1 8-oz. can
2 3-oz. boxes	Lemon or orange gelatin	1 3-oz. box
2 cups	Mild cheese, grated	1 cup
1½ cups	Mayonnaise	¾ cup
2 5¼-oz. cans	Evaporated milk	1 5¼-oz. can
1 cup	Pecans or walnuts	½ cup

Drain juice thoroughly from the pineapple and add enough water to make 2 cups of liquid for the larger quantity and 1 cup for the smaller quantity. Put the liquid in a small saucepan and bring to a boil. Remove from heat and pour over the gelatin in a mixing bowl. Stir to dissolve the gelatin and allow to cool for a few minutes. Add additional cold water, two cups for the larger quantity and one for the smaller. Stir in the crushed pineapple, cheese, mayonnaise, milk, and nuts. Chill until firm.

COOK J. R. Pittman   CHIEF P. O. Williams

Brunswick Stew

---

*When a local club or church barbecue is held "on the grounds"
in the city here, firefighters often are treated to a Georgia
favorite—Brunswick stew. Our original recipe for this delectable dish has been tested in our own kitchen and is adaptable
to the outdoor grill.*

YIELDS 6 TO 6½ QUARTS	INGREDIENTS	YIELDS 3 TO 3½ QUARTS
4 lbs.	Beef shoulder roast	2 lbs.
4 lbs.	Pork loin roast	2 lbs.
As needed	Cooking oil	As needed
2 2-lb. fryers	Chicken	1 2-lb. fryer
10	Soda crackers	5
2 cups	Beef broth	1 cup
2 cups	Pork broth	1 cup
2 cups	Chicken broth	1 cup
2 No. 2½ cans	Tomatoes	1 No. 2½ can
2	Onions	1
2 No. 303 cans	Corn	1 No. 303 can
1 cup	Catsup	½ cup
2 8-oz. cans	Tomato sauce	1 8-oz. can
3 to 4 Tbs.	Salt	1½ to 2 Tbs.
1 tsp. or to taste	Pepper	½ tsp. or to taste
4 Tbs.	Worcestershire sauce	2 Tbs.
4 Tbs.	Hot red-pepper sauce	2 Tbs.

The beef, pork, and fryers are to be cooked in separate pots. Brown
the beef first in a small amount of cooking oil over medium to high
heat. Add water to half cover the meat and cook, covered, for approximately 1½ hours over low heat. Brown the pork roast in the

same manner. Add water to half cover the meat and reduce the heat. Cover and cook for 1½ to 2 hours. Cut the fryers in halves or quarters and simmer over medium heat, covered, in just enough water to cover the chicken pieces. Remove all meat when cooked and allow to cool. Cut lean meat from the beef and pork roasts and run through a meat grinder, using the coarse blade so the meat will not be ground too fine. There should be about 6 cups of ground meat of each kind for 6 quarts of stew; 3 cups of ground meat of each kind for 3 quarts of stew. Add a small amount of fat—½ to 1 cup—to the meat grinder and run soda crackers through the grinder to thicken the stew. Bone the chicken and run the meat through the grinder. Add all other ingredients to a large pot along with ground meats and simmer together over low heat for 2 to 2½ hours.

Variation: After the beef and pork are partially cooked about an hour and before grinding, they may be grilled over hot charcoal for a smoky flavor. Chicken may be brushed with butter and barbecued on grill from the start. If meat is not grilled, smoky barbecue sauce may be substituted for catsup in the recipe.

COOK Roy Kite   CHIEF J. A. Landers

Fire-Alarm Chili

This is a favorite recipe of the men at No. 2 Station in College Park, Georgia. It is easy to prepare, almost totally devoid of any possible calamities—until it is attacked by the firefighters, that is.

SERVES 10	INGREDIENTS	SERVES 5
2 Tbs.	Margarine	1 Tbs.
2 lbs.	Ground beef	1 lb.
To taste	Salt and pepper	To taste
4 dashes	Worcestershire sauce	2 dashes
4 Tbs.	Chili powder	2 Tbs.
1 tsp.	Sugar	½ tsp.
2	Onions, chopped	1
2 No. 2 cans	Tomatoes	1 No. 2 can
2 No. 300 cans	Chili beans	1 No. 300 can

Melt the margarine in a large skillet. Crumble and brown the beef, adding salt and pepper to taste. Skim off excess fat. Add Worcestershire sauce, chili powder, sugar, and onions, and continue cooking until the onions are almost done. Chop the tomatoes and add them along with the beans. Bring the mixture to a boil, then lower heat to simmer for about 1 hour before serving.

COOK Roy Kite   CHIEF J. A. Landers

Country-Fried
Steak and Onions

The men at No. 2 Fire Station enjoy the rich, beefy gravy at least as much as the meat in this dish.

SERVES 8 TO 10	INGREDIENTS	SERVES 4 TO 6
4 lbs.	Round steak	2 lbs.
To taste	Salt and pepper	To taste
About 1½ cups	Flour	About ¾ cup
½ cup	Margarine	¼ cup
2	Onions, sliced	1
3 or more cups	Water	1½ or more cups
To taste	Additional salt and pepper	To taste

Cut the steak across the grain into 2″ strips. Salt and pepper the flour and press the seasoned flour into the meat. Melt the margarine in a large deep skillet and brown each piece of meat on both sides over medium heat. Remove steak from pan and reserve just enough fat for gravy. Add flour to fat in pan until the fat is absorbed (1 tablespoon flour for each tablespoon of fat) and let this become very brown. Add sliced onion, and then enough water to make gravy. Stir and allow to thicken. Gravy may be slightly thin at this stage but it will thicken as it continues simmering. Return steak to pan and correct seasoning. Cover the skillet, and reduce the heat to very low. Stir occasionally, scraping the bottom of the pan to keep the steak from sticking while simmering for 1 to 1½ hours.

COOK Roy Kite   CHIEF J. A. Landers

Lime Salad

This salad is served with the Christmas turkey at the College Park department. Dinner is served in the Engine Room of the No. 1 Fire Station. Fire trucks are moved outside, tables and chairs are brought in, and the families of all the firemen are invited for a feast. Presents are placed under the tree for the children and floral centerpieces from each table are later awarded to the wives. Although this is a delightful Christmas recipe, it is an attractive salad—cool and green—for any occasion.

SERVES 10 to 12	INGREDIENTS	SERVES 4 TO 6
8 ozs.	Cream cheese	4 ozs.
2 cups	Water	1 cup
2 pkgs.	Lime gelatin	1 pkg.
8	Marshmallows, chopped	4
1 cup	Heavy cream	½ cup
1 No. 2 can	Crushed pineapple	1 No. 1 can
1 cup	Pecans	½ cup

Soften cream cheese and set aside. Boil water and add to gelatin. Dissolve softened cream cheese in gelatin. While mixture is hot add marshmallows, and cool in refrigerator. Whip the heavy cream and fold it and the crushed pineapple (juice also) and pecans into gelatin mixture. Chill until firm and ready to serve.

COOK Roy Kite   CHIEF J. A. Landers

Roast Turkey

Turkey with savory dressing and giblet gravy is always served at the College Park fire department Christmas parties. The dressing is cooked separately from the turkey.

SERVES 14 TO 16	INGREDIENTS	SERVES 6 to 8
16 to 18 lbs.	Turkey	10 to 12 lbs.
2½ Tbs.	Salt	1½ Tbs.
¼ cup	Melted butter or margarine	⅛ cup

Clean the turkey and wipe dry. Rinse the giblets, put them in a saucepan with water, and simmer gently, covered, until tender. Reserve the broth in a large bowl. Meanwhile, put the turkey on a rack set in the bottom of a large roasting pan. Rub salt inside the turkey and under the skin at the neck. Secure the legs of the turkey with a cord. Brush melted butter or margarine all over the skin of the turkey. Pour water to depth of about 1½″ in bottom of pan under the rack. Cover the pan and bake in a 325° oven for 3½ to 4 hours for the smaller bird, or at 300° for 4½ to 5 hours for the larger bird. Baste every hour or so with the pan juices. When the skin is golden brown and the turkey is tender, remove from the oven and allow to cool slightly. Remove the bird to a serving platter and pour the pan juices into the bowl with the giblet broth: this liquid is used for the dressing and gravy (recipes follow). Add water if necessary. Chill the broth so that the congealed fat floats to the top for easy removal. Reserve fat for dressing.

COOK Roy Kite   CHIEF J. A. Landers

Turkey Dressing

SERVES 14 TO 16	INGREDIENTS	SERVES 6 TO 8
2 9" x 9" loaves	Cornbread (day-old)	1 9" x 9" loaf
4 slices	White bread	2 slices
1 cup	Cornflake crumbs	1/2 cup
6	Soda crackers	3
1/2 cup	Flour	1/4 cup
3/4 to 1 cup	Fat from turkey broth	Scant 1/2 cup
3 Tbs.	Butter, melted	1-1/2 Tbs.
4	Eggs	2
4 stalks	Celery	2 stalks
2	Onions	1
7 to 8 cups	Turkey and giblet broth	3 to 4 cups
2 tsp.	Salt	1 tsp.
2 tsp.	Basil	1 tsp.
2 tsp.	Thyme	1 tsp.
4 Tbs.	Sage	2 Tbs.

Crumble the cornbread into a large bowl. Make breadcrumbs from the slices of bread and mix them with the cornflakes, cracker crumbs, and flour. Add to the cornbread. Combine the fat skimmed off the cold turkey broth with the melted butter, and add to the dry ingredients. Beat the eggs, chop the celery and onions, and add to the dressing along with the cold turkey broth. Stir all ingredients together thoroughly. Sprinkle in the salt and other seasonings and mix again. The dressing should be of a medium consistency, neither dry or thin. If additional liquid is needed, add water or canned chicken broth. Pour into a large greased baking pan and bake, uncovered, at 350° until browned on top.

COOK Roy Kite   CHIEF J. A. Landers

Giblet Gravy

SERVES 14 TO 16	INGREDIENTS	SERVES 6 to 8
About 6 cups	Turkey and giblet broth	About 3 cups
¾ cup	Fat from turkey broth	½ cup
1 cup	Water	½ cup
½ cup	Flour	¼ cup
From a 16- to 18-lb. turkey	Giblets	From a 10- to 12-lb. turkey
3	Hard-boiled eggs	2
To taste	Salt and pepper	To taste

Heat the broth and fat in pan on top of stove. Make a thin paste of the water and flour in a cup, and pour slowly into broth. Continue to cook over medium heat, stirring constantly as the gravy thickens. Chop the giblets and the hard-boiled eggs, and add to the gravy. Season with salt and pepper and simmer over low heat until serving. If gravy is too thick, add more water or canned chicken broth.

COOK Roy Kite   CHIEF J. A. Landers

Buttermilk Candy
or Caramel Icing

My husband sometimes cooks up a batch of this candy for the men at No. 2 Station. But, despite the old saying, "a watched pot never boils," this one does boil and it really needs watching, and stirring, almost constantly.

YIELDS 40 1" SQUARES	INGREDIENTS	YIELDS 20 1" SQUARES
5 cups	Sugar	2½ cups
1 tsp.	Salt	½ tsp.
2 tsp.	Baking soda	1 tsp.
2 cups	Buttermilk	1 cup
2 tsp.	Vanilla	1 tsp.
4 Tbs.	Butter	2 Tbs.
1 cup	Nuts and raisins (optional)	½ cup

Mix sugar, salt, and baking soda together in a saucepan. Add the buttermilk and place on medium heat. Let boil gently, stirring constantly, until the mixture turns from a cream to a caramel color. Remove from heat and add butter and vanilla. Cool slightly; then beat until thickened. Nuts or raisins may be added at this stage. Pour the candy onto a buttered dish or platter. Cut into squares when the candy is completely cooled.

Note: Use the same ingredients to make a cake icing but do not beat as long or let it thicken as for candy.

Variations: If you omit baking soda and cook the mixture to the soft-ball stage, a white, buttermilk-flavored candy results. Coconut is a good addition to either version of the candy; add it with the nuts or raisins.

COOK Roy Kite   CHIEF J. A. Landers

Corn Fritters

YIELDS ABOUT 30	INGREDIENTS	YIELDS ABOUT 15
1 cup	Cream-style canned corn	½ cup
3	Eggs, separated	1 large
½ cup	Onion, chopped	¼ cup
1 Tbs.	Salt	½ Tbs.
1 Tbs.	Sugar	½ Tbs.
2 cups	Biscuit mix	1 cup
For deep frying	Cooking oil	For deep frying

Mix the corn, egg yolks, onion, salt, and sugar. Stir in biscuit mix. Beat egg whites in a separate bowl and fold into the corn batter. Drop by spoonfuls into hot, deep oil and fry until golden brown. You also may fry these as patties in a skillet using a smaller amount of oil.

COOK Clifford L. Todd   CHIEF L. L. Kenney

A Brief History of Firefighting in the United States

Colonial America's first fire departments were volunteer "bucket brigades," so called because buckets of water would be dipped from a source, usually a well, and passed hurriedly along a line of men to the fire. Each empty bucket would be rushed back to the source of water by the last man in line nearest the fire. The refilled buckets would continue down the line until the fire was extinguished. Often women and children would form a separate line to pass the empty buckets back to the water supply.

The serving of food and drink became a necessary part of the job of firefighting. The men were often seen grabbing the last bite of a favorite food while hurriedly leaving on a fire call. Some of the dishes prepared at the firehouses in those early days became so popular and well known that many companies were named for the specialties of their kitchens.

In the early 1800s men were alerted to trouble by the fire marshal, who blew a fire horn to summon help. The volunteer firemen pulled carts carrying gooseneck pumps, which they connected to a well to pump water by hand through a hose onto the fire.

The exhausting job of operating the pumps at a fire, the frequent battle with the elements in below-freezing temperatures, along with the disconcerting fights with rival companies, tried every man's strength to the point of collapse. Some companies therefore employed a steward whose job it was to hurry to each fire scene with an ample-sized keg on his shoulders. Three clearly marked spigots on the keg offered the firefighters a choice of restorative drinks for "medicinal purposes."

Neighbors near a fire scene offered hot coffee and food to the weary men and often after a well-fought fire the men were treated to a fine meal by the owner of a local eating place or tavern before they returned to the firehouse.

During the second half of the nineteenth century, horse-drawn steam engines began to be used. This was one of the most picturesque periods in fire department history. A steam fire engine was a colorful sight with smoke belching from its stack and two or three beautiful horses charging in front to a fire.

The transition to motor-driven fire apparatus was made in the early twentieth century. This marked the beginning of the development of the many specialized types of fire apparatus now in use. Today there are many well-equipped and high trained fire departments in this country—over 25,000 paid and volunteer fire departments, with more than 1,200,000 men and women in the fire service—a considerable advance in technology and specialization since the days of the bucket brigade.

from the
North Central States

[AKRON, OHIO]

Short-Ribs Special

As with most fire departments, cooking arrangements in Akron vary from station to station. At some stations the men take turns; others have a permanent cook. The wives help by sending in desserts. Firefighter Tom Labbe, who contributed this recipe, tells of a fellow at Station No. 5 who seems to celebrate about ten birthdays a year. His "birthdays" coincide with the arrival of any and all cakes at the firehouse. This has been going on for years but he's still only in his late thirties.

SERVES 12	INGREDIENTS	SERVES 6
6 to 7 lbs.	Beef short ribs	3 to 4 lbs.
About 1 cup	Flour	About ½ cup
To taste	Salt and pepper	To taste
½ cup	Cooking oil	¼ cup
2 4-oz. cans	Mushrooms	1 4-oz. can
1 cup	Celery, chopped	½ cup
½ cup	Green pepper, chopped	¼ cup
1 cup	Onions, chopped	½ cup
5 cups	Water	2½ cups
4	Beef-bouillon cubes	2

Dredge the ribs in flour seasoned with salt and pepper. Heat the oil in a skillet and brown the ribs on all sides. Place the browned ribs in a roasting pan with a tight-fitting cover, along with the mushrooms, chopped celery, green pepper, and onions. Pour over all the bouillon cubes dissolved in the hot water. Cover the pan and bake for 2½ to 3 hours at 350°. Then remove the ribs to a warm serving platter. Skim the excess fat from the gravy in roaster and discard. Serve the gravy over noodles, mashed potatoes, or rice.

COOK Tom Labbe   CHIEF Carl Best

Meat Loaf
Specialty

The fire chief in Chillicothe tells about the amazing talent of one of the cooks there. Dick Bost is self-taught and "can make a meal of nearly nothing, with the help of nearly none."

SERVES 8 TO 10	INGREDIENTS	SERVES 4 TO 6
3 lbs.	Ground beef	1½ lbs.
1 lb.	Sausage meat	½ lb.
3	Eggs, beaten	2
1 large	Onion	1 medium
1	Green pepper	½
10	Soda crackers	5
To taste	Salt and pepper	To taste
A few Tbs.	Catsup	A few Tbs.
½ cup	Water	¼ cup

In a large mixing bowl, combine the ground beef and sausage with the egg. Chop the onion and green pepper, and crush the crackers, and add them along with the salt, pepper, and enough catsup to bind to the meat mixture. Blend all ingredients thoroughly and put in a loaf pan. Add the water to the pan. Bake about 1½ hours at 350°, or until done.

Suggestion: Serve warm with vegetables or let the meat loaf cool and cut it into slices for sandwiches.

COOK Dick Bost   CHIEF Fred Krider

Hose-House
Beef Stew

SERVES 16 TO 18	INGREDIENTS	SERVES 6 to 8
6½ to 7 lbs.	Stew beef	2 to 2½ lbs.
30	Carrots	8
6	Onions	2
10 to 12	Potatoes	3 to 4
2 No. 2 cans	Green peas	1 small can
2 No. 2 cans	Corn	1 small can
2 No. 2½ cans	Tomatoes	1 No. 2 can
1½ cup	Flour or cornstarch	½ cup
To taste	Salt and pepper	To taste
1 large	Bay leaf	1 small
¾ tsp.	Oregano or basil	¼ tsp.

Pressurecook the beef in a small amount of water for about 20 or 25 minutes, or cook over medium heat in a heavy saucepan, covered, until tender (1½ to 3 hours). While the beef is cooking peel and chop the carrots, onions, and potatoes. Boil them in a large pot until half done (about 10 minutes) and drain, reservng the cooking water. When the beef is tender, remove from pot and reserve the broth. In a large roasting pan combine the beef, onions, carrots, potatoes, peas, corn, and tomatoes. Mix the flour or cornstarch with a small amount of water and slowly add this paste to the beef broth. Simmer the broth in a saucepan, stirring until thickened. Pour this gravy over the vegetables and beef in the roasting pan. Add enough water from the cooked vegetables to cover all ingredients. Add the salt, pepper, and other seasonings. Stir all the ingredients gently and bake, covered, in a 300° oven for 1 to 1½ hours.

COOK Donald Stacker   CHIEF Richard Moore

Easy
Peach Cobbler

This cobbler, like many of the firehouse dishes, is quick and easy to prepare. It is equally good when canned pineapple chunks are substituted for the canned peaches. For a thinner pudding, use more fruit juice.

SERVES 14 TO 16	INGREDIENTS	SERVES 4 TO 6
½ lb.	Butter	⅛ lb.
3 cups	Flour, self-rising	¾ cup
¾ tsp.	Salt	¼ tsp.
3 cups	Sugar	¾ cup
2¼ cups	Milk	Scant ⅔ cup
3 tsp.	Vanilla	1 tsp.
4 No. 2½ cans	Peaches	1 No. 2½ can

Melt the butter and pour it into a baking pan large enough to hold all ingredients. Add flour, salt, sugar, and vanilla. Stir in peaches, together with half the canned juice. Bake for about 1 hour at 350°, or until golden brown. Serve warm.

COOK Donald Stacker   CHIEF Richard Moore

Coffee Cake

---

*This is a good cake with morning coffee, but it's equally good
with milk or a bowl of chilled fruit.*

YIELDS FOUR 9″ PANS	INGREDIENTS	YIELDS TWO 9″ PANS
2 ¼-oz. pkgs.	Yeast	1 ¼-oz. pkg.
½ cup	Water	¼ cup
3 tsp.	Salt	1½ tsp.
½ cup	Sugar	¼ cup
1 cup	Milk	½ cup
3	Eggs	1 large
4¼ to 5 cups	Flour	2¼ to 2⅔ cups
¼ cup	Shortening	2 Tbs.

Topping

1 1-lb. box	Light brown sugar	½ 1-lb. box
½ cup	Butter	¼ cup
1 Tbs.	Flour	½ Tbs.
2 tsp.	Cinnamon	1 tsp.

Dissolve the yeast in warm water. Add salt and sugar to the warm
milk in a large mixing bowl. Beat the eggs and add them with the
yeast mixture to the milk. Beat thoroughly. Add half the flour and
stir well. Melt and add the shortening and then the rest of the
flour. Mix and stir until smooth, adding additional flour if necessary so the dough will not be sticky. Turn out on floured board
and knead for about 10 minutes until the dough is elastic and
light. Place in a greased bowl and turn the dough over. Set in a
warm place (about 80°) for 2 hours, or until the dough doubles
in size. Knead the dough down again; then let it rise for another
10 minutes. Shape the dough into round coffee cakes and place

on large cookie sheet or in 9″ cake pans. Let the cakes rise until doubled, about 1 hour. Mix the ingredients for topping and crumble over the cakes before baking. Do *not* knead down again. Bake in a preheated oven at 425° for 10 minutes, then turn down oven to 375° and bake about 10 minutes longer, or until topping is brown.

Note: Cinnamon and raisins can be added to dough before last rising. Nuts may be added to topping ingredients.

COOK Russell Shelton   CHIEF John J. Ziccardi

Deep-Fried Fish

This is a favorite recipe of the Fort Wayne fire department where Charles Imler cooks for his shift at Station No. 5. When Charles was a rookie fireman, he couldn't boil an egg, but over the years he has watched the cooking techniques of the old-timers at the station and is now quite a chef.

SERVES 10	INGREDIENTS	SERVES 5
5 lbs.	Lake perch or other similar fish	2½ lbs.
2 cups	Flour	1 cup
4	Eggs	2
2 cups	Milk	1 cup
2 cups	Beer	1 cup
2 cups	Cracker meal	1 cup
For deep frying	Cooking oil	For deep frying

Coat the fish with flour. Mix the eggs, milk, and beer and dip the floured fish into the mixture. Roll the fish in the cracker meal and deep fry in oil heated to 370°, a few pieces at a time.

Note: A typical meal on Friday night at No. 5 station might consist of lake perch, lima beans, salad, Twice-Baked Potatoes (next recipe), bread, and spice cake.

COOK Charles Imler   CHIEF Thomas Heckman

Twice-Baked Potatoes

Meal interruptions here, as in other fire departments, are an accepted part of the job. When an alarm rings, the food is forgotten. On one occasion cooking was cast aside so quickly that someone forgot to turn off the oven. When the men returned to the station, their meal was cooked well beyond the "golden brown" stage.

SERVES 12	INGREDIENTS	SERVES 6
12	Baking potatoes	6
5 to 6 Tbs.	Onions, minced	2 to 3 Tbs.
To taste	Salt and pepper	To taste
5 to 6 Tbs.	Butter	2 to 3 Tbs.
1 tsp.	Paprika	½ tsp.
½ cup	Sharp cheddar cheese, grated	¼ cup

Scrub and bake the potatoes until done. Remove from oven and allow to cool silghtly. Cut the potatoes lengthwise and dig the flesh out of the shell, being careful to retain shape of shell. Add the minced onions to the potatoes. Add butter and season with salt and pepper. Using a fork, mash the potatoes until soft and return to the shells. Sprinkle lightly with paprika. Slit the top of each stuffed potato lengthwise and put the cheese in the slits. Return to the oven on a cookie sheet and bake for 15 to 20 minutes in a 250° oven.

COOK Charles Imler   CHIEF Thomas Heckman

Flatterer
of the Palate

Each year in Indianapolis the fire and police departments hold a cake-baking contest at the Indianapolis Power and Light Company. In 1972 the fire department won the contest, and the cake recipe below won first prize for James Terry Short of Engine Company No. 17.

YIELDS FOUR 9″ LAYERS	INGREDIENTS	YIELDS TWO 9″ LAYERS
	Batter	
1⅓ cups	Shortening	⅔ cup
3⅓ cups	Sugar	1⅔ cup
6	Eggs	3
4½ cups	Cake flour	2¼ cups
½ cup	Cocoa	¼ cup
2 tsp.	Salt	1 tsp.
2½ tsp.	Baking soda	1¼ tsp.
½ tsp.	Baking powder	¼ tsp.
2⅔ cups	Water	1⅓ cup
2 tsp.	Vanilla	1 tsp.

In a mixing bowl, cream the shortening with the sugar, then beat in the eggs. In a separate bowl, sift together the flour, cocoa, salt, soda, and baking powder. Combine water and vanilla and add to shortening mixture, alternating with flour mixture and beating thoroughly after each addition. Pour in greased, floured cake pans. For 3 thinner layers, use 3 9″ cake pans. Bake at 350° for 30 to 35 minutes.

Filling and Topping

YIELDS FOUR 9″ LAYERS	INGREDIENTS	YIELDS TWO 9″ LAYERS
2 cups	Evaporated milk	1 cup
2 cups	Sugar	1 cup
6	Egg yolks	3
1 cup	Margarine	½ cup
2 tsp.	Vanilla	1 tsp.
4 cups	Coconut	2 cups
2 cups	Pecans, chopped	1 cup

Icing for Sides of Cake

6	Egg whites	3
2 cups	Shortening	1 cup
½ cup	Cocoa	¼ cup
2 tsp.	Vanilla	1 tsp.
2 1-lb. boxes	Powdered sugar	1 1-lb. box

Filling and Topping: In a saucepan combine the evaporated milk, sugar, egg yolks (reserving the whites), margarine, and vanilla. Stir over medium heat until thickened, about 12 minutes. Remove from heat and add coconut and chopped pecans. When cool spread between layers and on top of cake.

Icing for Sides of Cake: Beat the egg whites slightly. Add shortening, cocoa, vanilla, and sugar and whip until smooth.

COOK James Terry Short   CHIEF Richard Van Sant

Chicken
Paprikash

Usually there are twelve men to a shift here at Central Station. Six to ten men make up the cooking ring—three men cook and the rest wash dishes. This recipe has the unanimous approval of cooks and clean-up crew alike.

SERVES 12	INGREDIENTS	SERVES 6
4 large	Onions	2 large
4 Tbs.	Bacon fat or shortening	2 Tbs.
7 Tbs.	Paprika	3½ Tbs.
6 2- to 2½-lb. fryers	Chicken	3 2- to 2½-lb. fryers
To taste	Salt and pepper	To taste
As needed	Water	As needed
8	Chicken bouillon cubes	4
2 pts.	Sour cream	1 pt.
½ cup	Water	¼ cup
4 Tbs.	Flour	2 Tbs.

Chop and sauté the onions in bacon fat in a large frying pan. Off heat, add all but one tablespoon of the paprika to the onions and stir. Split the fryers into halves and put them into baking dishes or roasting pans. Spoon the onion-paprika mixture over the chicken and sprinkle with salt and pepper. Add water to depth of about 1″ to the pans and put in the bouillon cubes. Cover and bake for one hour at 350°. Remove chicken halves from broth in pans to cookie sheets or flat pans. Sprinkle them with the remaining paprika and return to the oven for 15 or 20 minutes, or until chicken is browned. Pour broth back into frying pan on top of the stove. Gradually stir in sour cream until smooth in texture.

Thicken sauce by making a thin paste of flour and water (2 tablespoons flour to ¼ cup water) and adding gradually to sour cream and broth over low heat. Serve warm in a sauceboat with the chicken and dumplings (recipe follows).

COOKS Ernie Donka, Hal Lieser, and Wayne Plant
CHIEF E. J. Bauman

Basic Dumpling Recipe

There is definitely an art to preparing dumplings. Once the dumplings are perfected, however, they go very well with the sour cream sauce in the preceding recipe.

SERVES 12 TO 14	INGREDIENTS	SERVES 6 TO 8
2 cups	Flour	1 cup
4 tsp.	Baking powder	2 tsp.
1 tsp.	Salt	½ tsp.
⅔ cup or less	Milk	⅓ cup or less
2	Eggs	1
2 qts.	Water or chicken broth	2 qts.

Mix together the dry ingredients. Blend in eggs and gradually add enough milk for a heavy drop batter. Drop the dough by teaspoons into gently boiling water or broth. Dip spoon in hot water each time to clean. Cook, uncovered, several minutes after dumplings rise to surface of the water. Test one dumpling by cutting in half. If center is dry, the dumpling is done. Remove them as they are done, and serve hot with Chicken Paprikash.

COOKS Ernie Donka, Hal Lieser, and Wayne Plant
CHIEF E. J. Bauman

Ship Wreck

The name of this recipe is inspired by one of the main ingredients, not by the outcome of the dish itself. For a ravenously hungry firehouse twelve, double the ingredients listed for 12 to 14 normal eaters.

SERVES 12 TO 14	INGREDIENTS	SERVES 6 TO 8
2 Tbs.	Shortening	1 Tbs.
2 lbs.	Ground beef	1 lb.
1	Green pepper, sliced	½
1 medium	Onion, chopped	1 small
2 No. 2 cans	Tomatoes	1 No. 2 can
23 ozs.	Tomato juice	12 ozs.
1½ Tbs.	Soy sauce	2 tsp.
½ lb.	Mushrooms, sliced	¼ lb.
2 8-oz. pkgs.	Baby sea shell macaroni	1 8-oz. pkg.
About 1½ cups	Cheddar cheese, grated	About ¾ cup
To taste	Salt and pepper	To taste

Preheat oven to 350°. Heat shortening in skillet and brown beef, sliced green pepper, and chopped onion. Combine tomatoes, tomato juice, soy sauce, and sliced mushrooms in roasting pan or large baking dish. Add ingredients from skillet, season, and bake for 1½ hours. Cook baby sea shell macaroni according to package directions and drain. Add to sauce ingredients in roaster or baking dish and cook, uncovered, for 10 minutes. Remove from oven, scoop aside part of the mixture and spread a layer of the cheddar cheese in the middle and a layer on top. Return to the oven for 10 minutes, or until the cheese is melted.

Suggestion: Serve with a green salad and garlic bread.

Note: The sauce for this dish is cooked in the oven before the macaroni is added, but it may also be prepared and simmered on top of the stove and later baked with a macaroni and cheese.

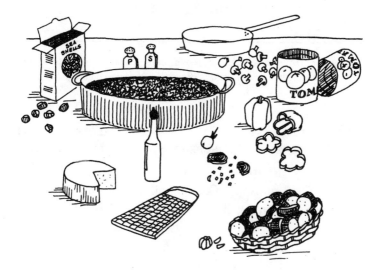

cooks All personnel   chief Willard Ashby

A Cake
from Kankakee

If you're in a cake-baking mood and want an easy-to-make recipe that will produce a differently delicious cake, try this favorite from Kankakee.

YIELDS TWO TUBE PANS OR BUNDT CAKES	INGREDIENTS	YIELDS ONE TUBE PAN OR BUNDT CAKE
1 cup	Sugar	½ cup
1½ cups	Cooking oil	¾ cup
2 boxes	Butter cake mix	1 box
8	Eggs	4
2 cups	Sour cream	1 cup
¾ cup	Additional sugar	6 Tbs.
2 tsp.	Cinnamon	1 tsp.

Preheat oven to 350°. Beat together the sugar and the cooking oil. Add cake mix and eggs, beating well after addition of each egg. Add sour cream and beat again. Mix additional sugar together with cinnamon, and sprinkle a small amount in the bottom of a greased cake pan. Pour in half of cake batter and top with half of the remaining cinnamon mixture (about 2½ tablespoons), then cover with the rest of the batter and sprinkle remaining cinnamon mixture on top. Bake 1 hour. Allow cake to cool before turning it out of pan.

COOK John Maass   CHIEF John Marquart

Sweet-Sour Short Ribs

This recipe is from the "Largest Village in the World."

SERVES 12	INGREDIENTS	SERVES 6
12 lbs.	Beef short ribs	6 lbs.
To taste	Salt and pepper	To taste
6 Tbs.	Shortening	3 Tbs.
To dredge ribs	Flour	To dredge ribs
3 cups	Onions, chopped	1½ cups
3	Garlic cloves, sliced	1

Sauce

3	Bay leaves	1
1 cup	Catsup	½ cup
¾ cup	Vinegar	⅜ cup
½ cup	Brown sugar	¼ cup
1 tsp.	Salt	½ tsp.
2 cups	Water	1 cup
About 4 Tbs.	Flour	About 2 Tbs.

Noodles

Season short ribs with salt and pepper, roll in flour, and brown well on all sides in hot shortening. Remove meat to a Dutch oven. Add chopped onions and sliced garlic to the skillet, cook until lightly browned, and add to short ribs. Combine bay leaves, catsup, vinegar, brown sugar, and salt to make a sauce, and pour over ribs. Cover and cook over low heat until tender, about 2½ to 3 hours. Remove ribs to a heated serving dish. Pour off excess fat

89

from gravy; stir in flour dissolved in water and cook sauce until thickened. Serve short ribs with buttered noodles topped with the gravy.

Note: Pot roast may be substituted for the short ribs.

COOK Gifford Gillingham   CHIEF Jerome P. Burke

Lasagne

This hearty dish is a real crowd-pleaser, not only at the fire-house, where it can satisfy the appetites of the hungriest crew, but as a main course when serving "fire buffs" at home. In the early days of volunteer firefighting, young men wanting to become firemen would often spend hours buffing the fire engines to a shine, just to be around the station until they could join the company—hence the name "buffs."

YIELDS 36 3″ x 3″ SERVINGS	INGREDIENTS	YIELDS 12 3″ x 3″ SERVINGS
6 lbs.	Ground beef	2 lbs.
3 cups	Onions, chopped	1 cup
16 cups (1 gal.)	Tomato sauce	5⅓ cups
3	Garlic cloves, minced	1
4 Tbs.	Sugar	1⅓ Tbs.
1 tsp.	Pepper	⅓ tsp.
3 tsp.	Salt	1 tsp.
2 tsp.	Anise seed	⅔ tsp.
3 Tbs.	Parsley, minced	1 Tbs.
3 tsp.	Basil	1 tsp.
2 Tbs.	Oregano	⅔ Tbs.
3 1-lb. boxes	Lasagne noodles	1 1-lb. box
4 lbs.	Mozzarella cheese, grated or sliced	1⅓ lbs.
8 ozs.	Parmesan cheese, grated	3 ozs.

Sauté the ground beef and onion in a large, heavy pan until meat is browned and onion is tender. Drain off grease and discard. Add tomato sauce, bring to boil, and add all of the herbs and spices. Reduce heat and simmer for 1 hour, uncovered, or until meat sauce has thickened. Prepare lasagne noodles according to package directions, taking care not to overcook them. When noodles are ready, drain and rinse in cold water. In the bottom of each baking pan (three 13″ x 9″ x 2½″ pans for the larger quantity; one for the smaller), spread a thin layer of meat sauce. On top of this place a double layer of noodles, then a second, heavier layer of meat sauce. On top of this place a layer of Mozzarella cheese, followed by a sprinkling of Parmesan cheese. Follow this with noodles, sauce and cheese in layers, making sure to retain enough Mozzarella for a thick topping layer. Bake for 30 to 45 minutes in a 325° oven.

COOK Dale Hendershot   CHIEF B. C. Grable

Fried Cabbage

Beloit has three cooks—one for each shift. The cooks buy all the food, and each man at the station pays $7.00 every two weeks for his meals. Although the favorite pastime of the men on each shift is badgering the cook, they still manage to offer tasty and economical menu items such as the one given here.

SERVES 8 TO 10	INGREDIENTS	SERVES 4 TO 5
2 lbs.	Ground beef	1 lb.
1	Green pepper, chopped	½
1 large	Onion, chopped	1 small
2 No. 2½ cans	Tomatoes	1 No. 2½ can
6 ozs.	Tomato paste	3 ozs.
1 large head	Cabbage	1 small head
To taste	Salt and pepper	To taste

In a large, heavy pan, brown the beef with the chopped green pepper and onion. Add tomatoes and tomato paste and bring to a boil. Chop or shred cabbage and add to ingredients in the pan. Reduce heat and simmer, covered, for 1½ hours. Season to taste before serving.

COOKS Gerald Buckley, Terry Moran, and Larry Allen
CHIEF H. V. Christiansen

Salmon Loaf with Pork

A portion of pork sausage added to a salmon loaf produces an unusual variation of an American stand-by.

SERVES 10 TO 12	INGREDIENTS	SERVES 3 TO 4
3 medium	Onions	1 small
½ stalk	Celery	2 Tbs.
4 1-lb. cans	Red salmon	1 1-lb. can
6	Eggs	2
3 Tbs.	Lemon juice	1 Tbs.
3 cups	Cracker crumbs	¾ cup
1 cup	Milk	¼ cup
1 cup	Liquid from salmon	¼ cup
1 lb.	Pork sausage	¼ lb.
1 tsp.	Salt	½ tsp.

Chop onions and celery. Bone salmon, reserving liquid from can. Mix all ingredients together. Form a loaf, and place it in a greased roasting pan. Cover and bake in a 350° oven, allowing 2 hours for the larger loaf and about 45 minutes for the smaller one, or until top is brown. Uncover and reduce heat to 300° during last 10 minutes of baking time.

COOK Emil J. Breidel   CHIEF Irvin Kahler

Deviled Chicken

When special guests are invited to partake of the firehouse fare in Milwaukee, they are often served this savory chicken, prepared by experienced cooks who have demonstrated their abilities not only in the firehouse kitchen, but also on a successful television series featuring firefighter chefs.

SERVES 8	INGREDIENTS	SERVES 4
2 Tbs.	Paprika	1 Tbs.
4 tsp.	Salt	2 tsp.
3 tsp.	Dry mustard	1½ tsp.
1 tsp.	Chili powder	½ tsp.
1 cup	Butter	½ cup
2 2- to 3-lb. fryers	Chicken, quartered	1 2- to 3-lb. fryers

Combine all seasonings in a cup and set aside. Melt butter in a shallow baking pan and turn quartered chicken in the butter until coated. Place chicken in pan with the skin side down. Cover pan with foil, and bake in a 400° oven for 30 minutes. Remove foil, turn chicken with skin side up, and sprinkle with combined seasonings. Cover and return to oven until chicken is tender, in about 30 minutes.

Suggestion: Garnish with tomato wedges and sprigs of parsley, or serve with sweet-sour green beans (recipe follows) and cranberry relish.

COOKS All personnel   CHIEF William Stamm

French-Cut Green Beans
with Sweet-Sour Sauce

Upon entering the world of culinary arts, firehouse-style, a Milwaukee firefighter is first detailed as a "helper." Basic training may include observing the preparation of this dish by one of the knowledgeable chefs here.

SERVES 8	INGREDIENTS	SERVES 4
4 strips	Bacon	2 strips
½ cup	Vinegar	¼ cup
½ cup	Water	¼ cup
½ cup	Sugar	¼ cup
2 tsp.	Cornstarch	1 tsp.
4 cups	Green beans, French-cut	2 cups

Fry bacon strips until crisp and drain on paper towel. Reserve several tablespoons of fat in the pan, and discard excess. Combine vinegar, water, and sugar, add to the reserved fat, and simmer for 3 minutes. In a cup or small bowl, mix a few tablespoons of this liquid with the cornstarch. Add this thin paste to ingredients in the skillet. Crumble bacon pieces into pan and simmer sauce for an additional 3 minutes to thicken. Pour over cooked and drained green beans and serve hot.

COOKS All personnel   CHIEF William Stamm

Sauerbraten

One of the chefs at headquarters station in downtown Milwaukee cooks for a 25-man shift. They chose this recipe as one of his best.

SERVES 15	INGREDIENTS	SERVES 5
10 lbs.	Beef chuck roast	3½ to 4 lbs.
1½ qts.	Wine vinegar	1½ pts.
3 qts.	Water	1 qt.
2 2½-oz. boxes	Pickling spice	⅔ of a 2½-oz. box
1	Lemon	⅓
3 lbs.	Onions	1 lb.
6 Tbs.	Shortening	3 Tbs.

Gravy

30	Ginger snaps	10
1 cup	Water	⅓ cup

Mix vinegar, water, and pickling spice in a large glass bowl or earthenware container. Cover meat with this mixture, and slice lemon and onion over it. Cover and allow to marinate for at least 36 hours, in the refrigerator. After it is ready, brown the beef in hot shortening in an open roaster over medium heat on top of the stove. Pour enough strained marinade into roaster to barely cover meat. Simmer, uncovered, over low heat, for 2½ hours, or until meat is tender. Remove meat to serving platter and allow to cool slightly before slicing. About 10 minutes before serving, soak ginger snaps in water and add to desired amount of broth for gravy in roaster. Bring to a boil, then serve immediately with sliced meat.

Suggestion: Potato or egg dumplings are recommended with this dish.

Note: Roast may be simmered in covered pan on top of stove. If this method is used, less marinade is put into pan—about 4 cups for larger and 2 cups for smaller roast. The meat should be turned once or twice during cooking.

COOK Elmer Kussrow   CHIEF William Stamm

Beer-Battered Chicken

The firefighters at Wauwatosa voted Roy Huebner as the chef to represent them with his favorite recipes. Here is a first-rate example of Roy's culinary art in the firehouse kitchen.

SERVES 8	INGREDIENTS	SERVES 4
2 fryers	Chicken	1 fryer
From 4 stalks	Celery leaves	From 2 stalks
1 large	Onion	1 small
To taste	Salt	To taste
For deep frying	Cooking oil	For deep frying

	Batter	
12 ozs.	Beer	8 ozs.
1½ cup	Flour	1 cup
1½ tsp.	Salt	1 tsp.
1½ tsp.	Sugar	1 tsp.
1½ tsp.	Baking powder	1 tsp.
1	Egg	1

Cut chicken into serving pieces, cover with water, and bring to a gentle boil. Add celery leaves, whole onion, and salt, and cook over medium heat for about 20 minutes. Remove chicken from broth and let cool. Mix batter ingredients in a large bowl. Heat cooking oil until it is very hot. Dip chicken in batter and deep fry until crisp and golden brown.

COOK Roy Huebner   CHIEF Lee R. Light

Cherry Torte

The firefighters in Wauwatosa take turns cooking. Each usually cooks for one month, but sometimes a chef is voted by popular demand to supervise the kitchen for an additional month. This dessert is one of their most popular recipes, courtesy of their favorite cook.

YIELDS TWO 9" PANS	INGREDIENTS	YIELDS ONE 9" PAN
2 cups	Sugar	1 cup
2 tsp.	Baking soda	1 tsp.
2 tsp.	Cinnamon	1 tsp.
2 cups	Flour	1 cup
2 tsp.	Baking powder	1 tsp.
2	Eggs, beaten	1
4 tsp.	Butter or margarine, melted	2 tsp.
2 No. 2 cans	Sour cherries	1 No. 2 can
2 cups	Pecans, chopped	1 cup

Sauce

1 cup	Sugar	½ cup
About 2 cups	Cherry juice	About 1 cup
4 tsp.	Cornstarch or flour	2 tsp.
¼ tsp.	Salt	⅛ tsp.

Whipped cream

Sift together the sugar, baking soda, cinnamon, flour, and baking powder in a large bowl. Combine beaten eggs and melted butter or margarine, and add to dry ingredients. Mix well. Drain cherries, reserving juice from can for sauce. Add cherries and chopped pecans to the batter. Stir lightly. Spread in greased cake pans and bake in a 350° oven for 35 to 40 minutes. Cool and cut into serving pieces.

Sauce: In a saucepan, combine sugar, cornstarch, salt, and reserved cherry juice and cook over medium heat until thickened. Pour over torte and top with whipped cream.

COOK Roy Huebner   CHIEF Lee R. Light

Cole Slaw

---

*This popular dish is often found on firehouse menus through-
out the country. The version here is favored by the firemen in
Winona, and uses onion, green pepper, and carrots.*

SERVES 10 TO 12	INGREDIENTS	SERVES 3 TO 4
1 3- to 4-lb. head	Cabbage	¼ of 3- to 4-lb. head
1 small	Onion	2 to 3 Tbs.
1 small	Green pepper	2 Tbs.
2	Carrots	1 small
½ cup	Sugar	2 Tbs.
2 heaping Tbs.	Celery seed	2 tsp.
2 cups	Mayonnaise	¼ cup

Shred or chop the cabbage. Mince onion and green pepper, and
toss with the cabbage. Shred carrots and add, along with sugar
and celery seed. Stir in mayonnaise to coat vegetables immediately before serving.

COOK George Hoeppner   CHIEF Ervin Laufenburger

Cucumber Salad

SERVES 10 TO 12	INGREDIENTS	SERVES 3 TO 4
8	Cucumbers	2
1 large	Onion	1 small
As needed	Salt	As needed
As needed	Water	As needed
1 cup	White vinegar	¼ cup
1 cup	Sugar	¼ cup
2 cups	Water	½ cup
To taste	Pepper	To taste

Peel and thinly slice cucumbers and onions. Make a medium brine by mixing salt and water (1 tsp. salt for each cup of water) and soak cucumber and onion in it for 1 to 1½ hours. Combine the vinegar, sugar, and water in a saucepan and cook over medium heat for 5 minutes. Allow this dressing to cool slightly, then place in freezer until it begins to set. Drain and rinse the cucumber and onion in cold water, then add them to the chilled vinegar dressing. Season with pepper. Refrigerate for 1 to 1½ hours before serving.

Note: For a stronger vinegar flavor, substitute additional vinegar for a portion of the water.

COOK George Hoeppner   CHIEF Ervin Laufenburger

Hot German
Potato Salad

SERVES 12	INGREDIENTS	SERVES 6
12	Potatoes	6
12 strips	Bacon	6 strips
⅔ cup	Bacon fat	⅓ cup
1½ cup	Onions, chopped	¾ cup
4 Tbs.	Flour	2 Tbs.
2 Tbs.	Sugar	1 Tbs.
1 Tbs.	Salt	1½ tsp.
1 tsp.	Celery seed	½ tsp.
To taste	Pepper	To taste
1½ cups	Water	¾ cup
1 cup	Wine or cider vinegar	½ cup

Boil potatoes in their skins until tender. Peel and cut them into thin slices. Fry bacon until crisp, and set it aside to drain. Reserve some of the bacon fat in the skillet, and sauté the chopped onions in it until they turn yellow. Stir in the flour, sugar, salt, celery seed, and pepper. Gradually add the water and vinegar. Bring to a boil and stir constantly for 1 minute. Pour this dressing over the potatoes. Crumble the reserved bacon and mix salad thoroughly. Cover and keep warm until ready to serve.

COOKS George Frank and Joe Helfrich   CHIEF Howard M. Goettsch

Applesauce
Meat Loaf

Most of the firefighters take turns as chef here, alternating on a monthly basis. A particularly good cook may stay on duty for a longer period. If, on the other hand, his food proves to be totally atrocious, he is deleted from the cooking roster, for the benefit of all concerned. The recipe below is from a cook on the roster, by the way.

SERVES 12	INGREDIENTS	SERVES 6
2 lbs.	Ground beef	1 lb.
1 lb.	Ground pork	½ lb.
1½ cups	Onions, minced	¾ cup
1 tsp.	Sage	½ to 1 tsp.
2 tsp.	Worcestershire sauce	1 tsp.
1 tsp.	Salt	½ tsp.
2 1-lb. cans	Applesauce	1 1-lb. can
2 cups	Bread crumbs	1 cup

Combine beef, pork, onion, sage, Worcestershire sauce, and salt and mix thoroughly. Add applesauce and bread crumbs and mix again. Pack lightly into a loaf pan and bake in 350° oven for 1 hour.

Note: Amount of sage may be varied to taste.

COOKS Most personnel   CHIEF Robert N. Dunphy

Ham Balls

This recipe was submitted by the chief in Dubuque who, for nine years of his fire service career, was also a firehouse chef.

YIELDS 36 TO 38 TO SERVE 10 TO 12	INGREDIENTS	YIELDS 18 TO 20 TO SERVE 4 TO 6
2 lbs.	Ground ham	1 lb.
2 lbs.	Ground pork shoulder	1 lb.
1 cup	Milk	½ cup
2 cups (about 64)	Soda crackers, crushed	1 cup (about 32)
2	Eggs	1

Sauce

3 cups	Brown sugar	1½ cups
2 tsp.	Dry mustard	1 tsp.
1 cup	Vinegar	½ cup
1 cup	Water	½ cup

Mix thoroughly the ham, pork, milk, crushed crackers, and eggs. Shape into meat balls about 2″ to 3″ in diameter and put into roasting pan or baking dish. Combine brown sugar, mustard, vinegar, and water and pour this sauce over ham balls. Bake, covered, for about ½ hour in a 350° oven, turn ham balls once, and continue baking for an additional ½ hour. Remove ham balls to a serving dish, pour sauce over them, and serve immediately.

COOK Robert N. Dunphy   CHIEF Robert N. Dunphy

Barbecued Rabbit

Although this recipe specifies rabbit, you'll find that spareribs, pheasant, or other meats are also delicious prepared in this tangy sauce.

SERVES 8	INGREDIENTS	SERVES 4
	Sauce	
1 cup	Catsup	½ cup
½ cup	Water	¼ cup
⅓ cup	Vinegar	⅙ cup
1 tsp.	Salt	½ tsp.
½ tsp.	Pepper	¼ tsp.
1 Tbs.	Paprika	½ Tbs.
1 Tbs.	Sugar	½ Tbs.
½ tsp.	Garlic salt	¼ tsp.
¼ cup	Butter	⅛ cup
1 Tbs.	Worcestershire sauce	½ Tbs.
1 medium	Onion, chopped	1 small
	Meat	
2 or 3 (allow ¾ to 1 lb. per person)	Young 2½- to 3-lb. rabbits, cut in serving pieces	1 or 2 (allow ¾ to 1 lb. per person)
½ cup	Shortening	¼ cup
½ cup	Flour	¼ cup
2 Tbs.	Paprika	1 Tbs.
½ tsp.	Pepper	¼ tsp.
½ tsp.	Salt	¼ tsp.
2 tsp.	Poultry seasoning	1 tsp.

Preheat oven to 350°. Combine catsup, water, vinegar, salt, pepper, paprika, sugar, and garlic salt in a roasting pan or baking dish with a cover. Add butter, Worcestershire sauce, and chopped onion. Cover and simmer sauce in the oven while preparing rabbit. Dredge rabbit pieces in flour seasoned with paprika, salt, pepper, and poultry seasoning. Brown the meat in heated shortening in a skillet, remove to roasting pan, and baste with sauce. Bake, covered, for 2 hours, or until tender.

COOK Patrick C. Akers   CHIEF Robert L. Keating

Pork Loin
Casserole

SERVES 12	INGREDIENTS	SERVES 4
12 large	Potatoes	4 large
12 large	Onions	4 large
12	Pork loin chops	4
3 10¾-oz. cans	Mushroom soup	1 10¾-oz. can
To taste	Salt and pepper	To taste
3 soup cans	Water	1 soup can

Peel and cut potatoes and onions in ¼″ slices. Arrange in alternate layers in a large, greased casserole dish. Place pork chops on top. Combine soup and water with salt and pepper in bowl or saucepan, and pour over all ingredients. Cover and bake at 300° for about 2 hours, removing cover during last ½ hour of cooking time to brown chops.

COOK Jerry Norton   CHIEF Williard Swoffer

Chicken
and Dumplings

*In Independence, the men pool their money to buy groceries.
The man who is known to do the best job of cooking the menu
decided upon is appointed chef for the day.*

SERVES 10 TO 12	INGREDIENTS	SERVES 4 TO 6
8	Chicken breasts	4
As needed	Water	As needed
½ lb.	Butter or margarine	¼ lb.
2 tsp.	Salt	1 tsp.
To taste	Pepper	To taste
2 cans (20)	Prepared biscuits	1 can (10)
1 cup	Evaporated milk	½ cup
About 12 cups	Chicken broth	About 6 cups

In a large pot or pan, cover chicken with water. Boil chicken over medium heat until tender, remove from pot, and set aside. Strain the broth and return it to pot, adding butter or margarine, salt, and pepper. Roll out the biscuits on floured board as thin as possible—about the size of a saucer—and cut them into 1″ strips. Bring broth to a boil and drop the dumpling strips one at a time into the pot, taking care to move the dumplings around so they won't stick together. When all the dumplings have been added to the broth, reduce heat to medium. Bone chicken, cut into bite-size pieces, and drop in with dumplings. Add evaporated milk and cook until the dumplings are done and the broth is thickened, about 15 to 20 minutes, stirring occasionally.

Note: Longer strips of dumplings may be cut in two.

COOK Lee Roy Whitson   CHIEF Williard Swoffer

Spanish Pork Chops

This easy-to-prepare dish, like so many firehouse recipes, cuts preparation time to a minimum—the idea being that there are many fire-related duties to perform that must always have priority.

SERVES 12	INGREDIENTS	SERVES 4
12	Pork chops	4
To taste	Salt and pepper	To taste
About 1 cup	Catsup	About ¼ cup
2 large	Onions	1 large
About 4 Tbs. per chop	Pickle juice from jar of sweet pickles	About 4 Tbs. per chop

Rub the pork chops with salt and pepper. Spread a tablespoon of catsup on one side of each pork chop. Place chops in a single layer in baking dish, with catsup side down. Spread an additional tablespoon of catsup on top side of each pork chop. Slice onions and place 2 slices on top of each chop. Pour sweet pickle juice over all to a depth of one-half the thickness of the chops. Bake uncovered in a 350° oven for 1 to 1½ hours. After first half hour of baking time, turn chops over and baste with juice from dish, rearranging onion slices on top.

COOK Eugene Knight   CHIEF Williard Swoffer

Filleted Breast
of Goose or Duck

This basic method for preparing goose or duck may also be used with chicken or other fowl.

SERVES 8	INGREDIENTS	SERVES 4
4 large	Geese or duck breasts	2 large
To taste	Salt or pepper	To taste
½ cup	Flour	¼ cup
About ½ cup	Shortening	About ¼ cup

Fillet the breasts of fowl into ¼" slices. Salt and pepper to taste and dredge in flour. Heat shortening in skillet and fry fillets, turning to brown on both sides, as you would pan-broil beef steak.

COOK Dennis Conner   CHIEF Williard Swoffer

Pork Chops
with Wild Rice

These firehouse chefs presented us with a tasty one-dish recipe that's a snap to make—it's prepared, cooked, and served in the same baking dish.

SERVES 12	INGREDIENTS	SERVES 6
2 6-oz. boxes	Long grain and wild rice mix	1 6-oz. box
2 10½-oz. cans	Cream of mushroom soup	1 10½-oz. can
2½ cups	Water	1¼ cups
2 4-oz. cans	Mushrooms	1 4-oz. can
12	Pork chops	6
To taste	Salt and paprika	To taste

Combine the uncooked rice with the soup and water in a baking dish. Mix with the mushrooms. Arrange the pork chops on top and sprinkle with salt and paprika. Cover and bake 1 hour and 20 minutes in a 350° oven.

Note: Pork chops may be browned in a skillet before baking.

COOKS Archie Strawn and Arch Pollock   CHIEF Max Woods

Baked Steak

Firemen are thinking ahead when they prepare one-dish meals such as this . . . not only to the possibility that they may be called to a fire, but even farther ahead to the chore none of us likes—the clean-up job after a meal.

SERVES 8 TO 10	INGREDIENTS	SERVES 4 TO 6
4 to 5 lbs.	Round steak	2 to 3 lbs.
3 Tbs.	Shortening	1½ Tbs.
To taste	Salt and pepper	To taste
½ cup	Flour	¼ cup
8 to 10	Carrots, diced	4 to 5
2 stalks	Celery, chopped	1 stalk
10	Potatoes, quartered	5
2 pkg.	Onion soup, dehydrated	1 pkg.
3 cups	Water or beef broth	1½ cups
4 Tbs.	Flour	2 Tbs.

Heat the shortening in a skillet. Dredge the steak in flour seasoned with salt and pepper, and brown both sides in skillet. Place browned steak in a large roasting pan and add diced carrots, chopped celery, quartered potatoes, sprinkling dehydrated onion soup over all. Heat water or broth in skillet used for browning the meat, scraping up all the brown bits stuck to pan, and add these pan juices to the roaster to insure stock for gravy. Sprinkle additional salt and pepper over all. Cover and bake until tender in a 350° oven, or about 1½ hours. Serve from baking dish or remove meat and vegetables to serving platter. Thicken broth in pan by making a thin paste of water and several tablespoons of flour in a cup, and stirring it gradually into the broth. Heat until gravy thickens.

Suggestions: Mushrooms or mushroom gravy mix may be substituted for onion soup mix. For a spicy dish, add one or two red peppers along with the onion soup.

COOK Frank P. Shortino   CHIEF John Waas

Meat Balls and
Tomato Sauce over Rice

For a quick, easy, and tasty rice dish this recipe is hard to beat. The men in Springfield serve it over rice, but the meat balls and sauce are also good over spaghetti or tiny egg noodles.

SERVES 12	INGREDIENTS	SERVES 6
2 pkgs.	Onion soup, dehydrated	1 pkg.
2½ cups	Water	1¼ cups
4 8-oz. cans	Tomato sauce	2 8-oz. cans
2 lbs.	Ground beef	1 lb.
1 tsp.	Garlic salt	½ tsp.
2 tsp.	Sugar	1 tsp.
¼ to ½ tsp.	Thyme	⅛ to ¼ tsp.
To taste	Pepper	To taste
	Rice	

Combine onion soup, water, and three-quarters of the tomato sauce in a covered saucepan, bring to a boil, then lower heat to simmer for 10 minutes. Mix together meat, seasonings, and remaining tomato sauce. Shape into walnut-size balls and drop into sauce. Simmer gently, uncovered, for 30 minutes, turning meat balls occasionally. Serve over fluffy cooked rice.

COOKS All personnel   CHIEF Ray Craig

Chicken
and Dressing

For an easy way to prepare chicken and dressing, try this specialty from Overland Park.

SERVES 10 TO 12	INGREDIENTS	SERVES 5 TO 6
2 2½- to 3-lb. fryers	Chicken, cut into serving pieces	1 2½- to 3-lb. fryer
1½ cups	Flour	¾ cup
To taste	Salt and pepper	To taste
½ cup	Shortening	¼ cup
2 8-oz. pkg.	Cornbread stuffing	1 8-oz. pkg.
4 10½-oz. cans	Cream of chicken soup	2 10½-oz. cans
2 soup cans	Water	1 soup can
4 tsp.	Minced dried onions	2 tsp.
½ tsp.	Celery salt	¼ tsp.
⅔ tsp.	Sage	⅓ tsp.

Dredge chicken pieces in flour and seasonings and brown them in heated shortening. In a bowl mix cornbread stuffing and half of cream of chicken soup that has been diluted with water. Add onions, celery salt, and sage. Spoon the stuffing into a greased Dutch oven. Place browned chicken pieces on top of stuffing and pour remaining half of undiluted soup over chicken. Cover and bake in a 350° oven for 1 hour.

COOK Jim McGee   CHIEF James G. Broockerd

Crappie (Fish)
Delight

A crappie is a small sunfish found in the central U.S. A lightly crisp and delectable crust is obtained when the fish are fried in the easy-to-prepare batter given below.

SERVES 6 TO 8	INGREDIENTS	SERVES 3 TO 4
4 cups	Pancake mix	2 cups
20 ozs.	7-Up	10 ozs.
To taste	Salt and pepper	To taste
4 lbs.	Crappie fillets	2 lbs.
For deep frying	Cooking oil	For deep frying

Combine the pancake mix with the 7-Up. Salt and pepper fillets and dip in batter. Deep fry in hot oil until golden brown.

Suggestion: For an interesting variation, substitute a mixture of half corn meal and half flour for the pancake mix.

COOKS All personnel   CHIEF Floyd H. Dibbern

Moose Rolls

Since no moose steaks were readily available, we tested this recipe with beef steaks which proved to be quite good, so you really don't have to put on your hunting boots and go stalking for moose to try it.

SERVES 12	INGREDIENTS	SERVES 6
4 large (6 lbs.)	Sirloin steaks of moose	2 large (3 lbs.)
4 Tbs.	Prepared mustard	2 Tbs.
To taste	Salt and pepper	To taste
To taste	Garlic salt	To taste
2	Onions	1
12 strips	Bacon	6 strips

Lay steaks out flat and cut into 1½″ strips. Spread the meat with mustard and season with salt and pepper. Cut onions into rings and cover the steak strips with them. Sprinkle lightly with garlic salt. Roll up the strips of meat, wrap a slice of bacon around each, and secure each bacon-wrapped roll with a toothpick. Place in a skillet and brown on all sides, turning frequently. Reduce heat, cover, and cook until tender.

cooks All personnel   chief Floyd H. Dibbern

Tony's Italian Meat Balls
and Spaghetti Dinner

After the hungry men at the Omaha firehouse dig into this spaghetti dinner, not a drop of sauce or a strand of spaghetti is ever left over.

SERVES 10 TO 12	INGREDIENTS	SERVES 5 TO 6
	Sauce	
2 large	Onions	1 large
2	Green peppers	1
6 Tbs.	Cooking oil	3 Tbs.
1 lb.	Ground beef	½ lb.
4 6-oz. cans	Tomato paste	2 6-oz. cans
2 Tbs.	Salt	1 Tbs.
2 Tbs.	Sugar	1 Tbs.
2 Tbs.	Kitchen Bouquet (or equivalent)	1 Tbs.
2 Tbs.	Chili powder	1 Tbs.
½ tsp.	Cumin	¼ tsp.
6 dashes	Hot red-pepper sauce	3 dashes
12 tomato paste cans	Water	6 tomato paste cans
	Meat Balls	
2 lbs.	Ground beef	1 lb.
2	Eggs	1
To bind	Bread or cracker crumbs	To bind
½ tsp.	Garlic salt	¼ tsp.
To taste	Pepper	To taste
	Spaghetti Parmesan cheese	

Chop onions and peppers and sauté in cooking oil until lightly brown. Crumble beef into onions and pepper and brown. Add remaining sauce ingredients, stir well, bring to boiling point, then lower heat to simmer. Meanwhile, prepare meatballs by combining ground beef, eggs, bread crumbs, and seasonings, rolling this meat mixture into 1″ balls, and adding the balls to the simmering sauce. Simmer sauce and meat balls for about 2 hours. Prepare spaghetti according to package directions, drain, and rinse with warm water. Serve meat balls and sauce over spaghetti and sprinkle with Parmesan cheese.

COOK Don Dougherty   CHIEF Vernon L. Van Scoy, Jr.

Green Pepper Sauce over
Italian Sausage Sandwiches

Charcoal grilling is a specially good way to prepare Italian sausages. Grill them whole, then slice and serve covered with this rich tomato and pepper sauce.

SERVES 12	INGREDIENTS	SERVES 6
4 tsp.	Olive oil	2 tsp.
2 No. 2½ cans	Stewed tomatoes	1 No. 2½ can
2 tsp.	Basil	1 tsp.
½ tsp.	Garlic salt	¼ tsp.
½ tsp.	Crushed red peppers	¼ tsp.
To taste	Salt	To taste
2	Green peppers	1
To serve 12	Italian sausages	To serve 6
12	Sesame-seeded buns	6

In advance, start outdoor charcoal fire to grill Italian sausages. Heat the olive oil in a skillet and add the canned tomatoes, basil, garlic salt, crushed red pepper, and salt to taste. Simmer this mixture, stirring, until tomatoes cook to a purée, about 20 minutes. Chop the green peppers and add to the tomato sauce. Cook over low heat, stirring often, for an additional 20 to 30 minutes, or until most of the water has evaporated and the sauce is very thick so that it almost sticks to the pan. Grill whole sausages until done. Slice sesame-seeded buns in half and toast on cut side. Split sausages lengthwise, place on buns, and cover generously with green pepper sauce before serving.

COOK Don Dougherty   CHIEF Vernon L. Van Scoy, Jr.

Smoky's
Special Bar-B-Q Sauce

This sauce can be stored in the referigerator for several weeks. It has many uses, and is especially good with roast beef or spareribs.

YIELDS ABOUT ONE GALLON	INGREDIENTS	YIELDS ABOUT ONE QUART
1 gal.	Catsup	1 qt.
5 ozs.	Worcestershire sauce	1½ ozs.
To taste	Celery salt	To taste
1 cup	Brown sugar	¼ cup
From 1 lemon	Lemon juice	From ¼ lemon
1 tsp.	Cumin	¼ tsp.
1 tsp.	Curry powder	¼ tsp.
Several dashes	Red pepper	Dash or two
8	Garlic cloves	2

Mince garlic cloves. Stir together all ingredients in a large, deep kettle. Simmer over low heat, stirring occasionally, until sauce thickens, for about 1 hour. Cool and store in covered containers in the refrigerator until ready to use.

COOK Don Dougherty   CHIEF Vernon L. Van Scoy, Jr.

Beef Stew
and Dumplings

*A firefighter could not scale ladders, wield fire axes, or lay lines
of hose with the meager energy supplied by a light luncheon
diet. The food must be hearty and filling, like this favorite of
the men in Aberdeen.*

SERVES 8 TO 10	INGREDIENTS	SERVES 4 TO 6
4 lbs.	Roast beef or stew beef	2 lbs.
To taste	Salt and pepper	To taste
4 Tbs.	Shortening	2 Tbs.
10 cups	Water	5 cups
4 large	Potatoes	2 large
2	Onions	1
2 Tbs.	Cornstarch or flour	1 Tbs.
1 cup	Water	½ cup
2 tsp.	Kitchen Bouquet (or equivalent)	1 tsp.
2 cups	Biscuit mix	1 cup
⅔ cup	Milk	⅓ cup

Cut roast or stew beef into bite-size chunks and season with
salt and pepper. Heat shortening in a large pot and add meat.
When beef is browned well, add water. Cover the pan and simmer
for 1 hour. While beef is cooking, quarter the potatoes and onions
and add to the stew pot. Continue to simmer until done, for about
2 hours. In a cup, mix the cornstarch or flour with water and add
this thin paste slowly to the stew for thickening. Add Kitchen
Bouquet and taste for seasoning. Mix biscuit mix with milk and,

use a teaspoon dipped in water, gently place dumplings about 1″ in diameter on top of simmering stew. Remove cover from pan for 10 minutes, then replace it and simmer for 15 minutes more before serving.

COOK Frank Fryer   CHIEF Earl Hood

Hunter's Stew

A hearty one-dish meal that makes you realize the hunt is over: you've found a great appetite-pleaser in Sioux Falls.

SERVES 10 TO 12	INGREDIENTS	SERVES 5 TO 6
3 lbs.	Stew beef	1½ lbs.
To taste	Salt and pepper	To taste
About 1 cup	Flour	About ½ cup
8 Tbs.	Shortening	4 Tbs.
2	Onions	1
4 No. 2 cans	Tomatoes	2 No. 2 cans
1 head	Cabbage	½ head
1	Green pepper	½
2 large pkgs.	Mixed vegetables, frozen	1 large pkg.
4 cans (40)	Buttermilk biscuits	2 cans (20)

Cube stew beef. Season and flour, fry in shortening until well browned, and remove to a roasting pan or large baking dish. Chop the onions, cabbage, and green pepper and add to meat with tomatoes and frozen vegetables. Add more salt and pepper to taste and stir all ingredients. Cover and bake in a 350° oven for 2 to 2½ hours. Remove the roaster from the oven and place the separated biscuits on top of stew. Bake 10 minutes, uncovered, at 400°, or until biscuits are browned.

COOK James L. Fink   CHIEF Burdette Sheldon

Tossed
Fruit Salad

The recipe for the favorite salad of the firemen in Minot originally belonged to the chef's family.

SERVES 16	INGREDIENTS	SERVES 8
4	Apples	2
4	Pears	2
2 large	Oranges	1 large
2 cups	Seedless grapes	1 cup
1 cup	Purple grapes	½ cup
6	Bananas	3
1 cup	Walnuts	½ cup
1½ to 2 cups	Mayonnaise	1 to 1½ cups
A few Tbs.	Milk or cream	A few Tbs.
To taste	Sugar	To taste
2 heads	Lettuce	1 head

Prepare all fruits: Dice unpeeled apples. Peel and dice the fresh pears. Cut the oranges and remove sections, discarding pulp and seeds. Cut seedless grapes in half. Cut purple grapes in half and remove seeds. Slice the bananas. In a large bowl, mix all the fruits and the walnuts. Add a little milk or cream to thin the mayonnaise, then add a little sugar to lightly sweeten it to taste. Add dressing to the fruit and toss. Serve on lettuce leaves, which have been washed, dried, and refrigerated for crispness.

COOK Jerald L. Fuchs   CHIEF Gilbert C. Malek

Firehouse Cooks–
from
Sidekick
to
Veteran Chef

One of the first things a rookie learns is that in order to eat at the firehouse, he must learn to cook. Some future chefs are introduced slowly to the culinary art, first assigned as helpers to observe the veteran chefs and their techniques. Other new firefighters, however, receive no apprenticeship and are put on the job in the kitchen rather abruptly—with the sudden knowledge that they must feed and please a large number of men. In such situations, calamities often occur, such as the time a rookie was told to boil

potatoes and forthwith dutifully dumped the potatoes—unpeeled and unwashed—into a pot of water. (We've also heard the story about the anonymous firehouse recruit whose pancake batter turns to a powerful mortar unless it's stirred constantly.) Apprentices in the firehouse kitchen are always advised to inform the men prior to mealtime what they are about to eat, since first attempts at specialized dishes aren't always recognized. Stories of early experiences become enlarged and widespread and it's often said that until the new cook proves himself worthy of the title of "chef," he is expected to supply digestive aids along with his meals.

Since all firehouse chefs are distinguished by a lack of pretention, the antics are not confined to the beginners. Many of the most experienced and established firefighter-cooks have developed their own unique kitchen habits. One former navy cook, now in full control of the situation in his firehouse kitchen, prepares a peculiarly delicious meat loaf by half-submerging it in water before baking it. A chef in Nebraska, after a good bit of experimentation in his culinary "lab," has created a secret formula for chili that, even in its milder version, is guaranteed to do wonders for a head cold.

When a firehouse chef in Kansas misplaced his rolling pin while preparing pie crust, he merely substituted a quart-size vinegar bottle and proceeded with the pastry-making, citing the "field expediency" learned during a recent stint in the army for his ability to make workable substitutions in times of kitchen crisis.

In Arkansas, a cook whose specialties are stews and soups finds it the most advantageous method to simply find the "biggest kettle in the firehouse kitchen" and "throw the vegetables in with the meat"—from a safe distance, we assume. Firehouse chefs are notorious for being undaunted by the rigors of recipes or the complexities of ingredients when preparing their meals, and have proved to be as ingenious and courageous in their methods of food preparation as in their primary job.

from the
South Central States

Sweet 'Tater
Casserole

Lemony tartness and sugar-honey sweetness lend taste-appeal to this southern specialty from Birmingham's firehouse kitchen. The cook also adds a little dry mustard to the casserole for an additional slight tanginess. "Be careful not to burn the 'mellers,'" advises the Birmingham Fire Prevention Bureau.

SERVES 10 TO 12	INGREDIENTS	SERVES 5 TO 6
6	Sweet potatoes	3
½ tsp.	Salt	¼ tsp.
3 Tbs.	Butter or margarine	1½ Tbs.
1 tsp.	Cinnamon	½ tsp.
1 cup	Granulated or brown sugar (or combination)	½ cup
From ½ lemon	Lemon juice	From ¼ lemon
2 Tbs.	Honey or molasses	1 Tbs.
¼ tsp.	Dry mustard	⅛ tsp.
A few Tbs.	Milk, or juice from drained pineapple	A few Tbs.
1 No. 2 can	Crushed pineapple, drained (optional)	1 No. 1 can
1 1½-oz. box	Raisins (optional)	3 Tbs.
To cover dish	Marshmallows	To cover dish

Wash potatoes, wrap in foil, and bake in 350° oven for 1 hour, or until soft when pierced with a fork. Peel potatoes while still warm and mash them with a fork in a large bowl. Add salt, butter, cinnamon, sugar, lemon juice, honey or molasses, and dry mustard. Beat on low speed with electric mixer until light, adding a bit of milk or juice from drained pineapple if potatoes are too dry. Fold in drained pineapple and raisins. Spoon mixture into a greased baking dish, cover the top with marshmallows and bake at 350° for 15 to 20 minutes, or until marshmallows melt and turn golden brown.

Skillet-Baked Corn Bread

Add cracklings to this fine corn bread recipe for a traditional Southern dish.

SERVES 12 TO 15	INGREDIENTS	SERVES 4 TO 6
¾ cup	Bacon drippings or shortening	¼ cup
3½ cups	Self-rising corn meal	1 heaping cup
1½ cups	Self-rising flour	½ cup
1 tsp.	Salt	⅓ tsp.
About 3 cups	Buttermilk	About 1 cup
2	Eggs	1

In a 10″ iron skillet, either cook the bacon for fat or heat the shortening. Do not skimp here as this will give the bread a delicious crust. Combine corn meal, flour, salt, milk, and eggs and beat until smooth. Remove about half of the heated fat from skillet and blend into corn bread mixture. Stir vigorously. Pour batter into the hot skillet and bake in 400° oven for about 30 minutes. Place on lower oven rack or under broiler to brown on top.

COOK John Harris   CHIEF John L. Swindle

Beef and Vegetable Soup

Packaged convenience foods and home-prepared ingredients are simmered together to make a good-tasting soup from Tuscaloosa's firehouse kitchen.

SERVES 10 TO 12	INGREDIENTS	SERVES 4 TO 6
4 lbs.	Ground beef or stew beef	2 lbs.
2 Tbs.	Cooking oil	1 Tbs.
1 1-lb. pkg.	String beans, frozen	½ lb.
1 1-lb. pkg.	Peas, frozen	½ lb.
2	Onions	1
2 No. 2 cans	Tomatoes	1 No. 2 can
1 cup	Catsup	½ cup
1 lb.	Potatoes	½ lb.
1 Tbs.	Hot red-pepper sauce	½ Tbs.
1 lb.	Carrots, frozen or canned	½ lb.
2	Beef bouillon cubes	1
To taste	Salt and pepper	To taste

Brown the beef in oil in a frying pan, meanwhile chopping the onions and dicing the potatoes. Combine all vegetables in a large pot, adding water as required for soup. Add the browned beef along with several tablespoons of the oil from the frying pan to the vegetables. Season with catsup, hot red-pepper sauce, salt, pepper and beef bouillon cubes. Simmer together until all ingredients are done, adding additional water as needed.

COOKS All personnel   CHIEF W. P. Callahan

Chicken
and Vegetables

SERVES 12	INGREDIENTS	SERVES 6
4 2½- to 3-lb. fryers	Chicken	2 2½- to 3-lb. fryers
To taste	Salt and pepper	To taste
6 large	Potatoes	3 large
8	Carrots	4
4 stalks	Celery	2 stalks
6 large	Onions	3 large
8 Tbs.	Margarine	4 Tbs.
4 10½-oz. cans	Golden mushroom soup	2 10½-oz. cans
2 10½-oz. cans	Water	1 10½ -oz. can

Season either whole or cut-up fryers with salt and pepper. Place chicken in a large roasting pan. Chop potatoes, carrots, celery, and onions and arrange around chicken. Melt the margarine and pour it over the chicken. Add salt and pepper to the vegetables. Combine soup and water, and pour diluted soup over the chicken and vegetables. Cover and bake at 350° for about 1½ hours.

Notes Cream of mushroom or cream of chicken soup may be substituted for golden mushroom soup.

COOK Gary J. Eaton   CHIEF A. G. Sumrall

French-Italian
Shrimp and Macaroni

This recipe includes a slow-simmering sauce which requires about four hours of cooking time to perfect the flavor and consistency.

SERVES 12	INGREDIENTS	SERVES 6
4	Onions	2
1	Green pepper	½
4 Tbs.	Cooking oil	2 Tbs.
4 15-oz. cans	Tomato sauce	2 15-oz. cans
2 12-oz. cans	Tomato paste	1 12-oz. can
2 for each can of tomato sauce and paste	Water	2 for each can of tomato sauce and paste
2½ Tbs.	Oregano	1¼ Tbs.
2	Bay leaves	1
2 Tbs.	Basil	1 Tbs.
1 cup	Parmesan cheese	½ cup
4 Tbs.	Garlic juice	2 Tbs.
½ of 9-oz. can	Italian bread crumbs	¼ of 9-oz. can
3 lbs.	Shrimp	1½ lbs.

Shell macaroni

Chop onions and green pepper and sauté in heated cooking oil. Add tomato sauce, tomato paste, and water. Stir well, and add oregano, bay leaves, basil leaves, Parmesan cheese, garlic juice, and bread crumbs. Simmer about 4 hours, stirring occasionally. Add shrimp during last 45 minutes of cooking time. Meanwhile cook macaroni until firm and chewy, then drain and rinse with warm water. Add to the sauce, stir over low heat until macaroni is well mixed.

Suggestion: Spread garlic butter on sliced French bread and bake until golden brown. Serve hot as an accompaniment to this dish.

COOK Julius (Scotter) Taranto   CHIEF Frank Gabrich

Firehouse Roast

The firehouse chef who sent us this recipe had never written one of his specialties down on paper before, and admits to having made several false starts before mailing the final draft. His efforts proved very effective.

SERVES 12	INGREDIENTS	SERVES 6
6 lbs.	Beef roast, chuck, shoulder, or sirloin tip	3 lbs.
To taste	Salt and pepper	To taste
1 pkg.	Dehydrated onion soup	½ pkg.
4 ozs.	Steak sauce	2 ozs.

Gravy

	Juices from roast	
1 pkg.	Dehydrated onion soup	½ pkg.
3 Tbs.	Flour	1½ Tbs.
As needed	Water	As needed

Place roast on heavy duty aluminum foil and season with salt and pepper to taste. Pour dehydrated onion soup mix over meat, add steak sauce, and seal foil. Put roast in a pan and bake in a 350° oven 2½ to 3½ hours (35 minutes per pound of meat), or until tender. To prepare gravy, combine meat juices and additional onion-soup mix. Add a thin paste mixed from the flour and water, and cook until gravy thickens.

COOK Henry E. Riley   CHIEF Jerry B. Black

40 Cents' Worth of Peas
and 7 Dollars' Worth of Ham

Nothing could be tastier in the state of Mississippi than this firehouse favorite. Serve it with stewed or candied tomatoes and a generous portion of hot, buttered cornbread.

SERVES 12 TO 15	INGREDIENTS	SERVES 5
3 lbs.	Dried black-eyed peas	1 lb.
8 to 9 quarts	Water	2½ to 3 quarts
1 Tbs.	Salt	1 tsp.
6 to 8 lbs.	Ham	2 lbs.
1 medium	Onion	1 small

Boil the water in a large pot, and add salt and peas that have been picked and washed. Reduce heat. Dice ham in 1″ to 2″ cubes and add to peas, along with a whole onion. Cook over low heat until peas and ham are done.

Note: The amount specified for peas is for generous one-cup servings. For smaller servings, use only half of the specified amounts.

COOK Henry E. Riley   CHIEF Jerry B. Black

Cream-Cheese Pie

Crushed pineapple, fresh or frozen strawberries, peaches, or cherry-pie filling may be used as alternates for the blueberries in this dessert recipe.

SERVES 12	INGREDIENTS	SERVES 6
2 or 3 9" shells	Pie pastry, frozen	1 9" shell
8 ozs.	Cream cheese	4 ozs.
1 1-lb. box	Confectioners sugar	½ 1-lb. box
2 envelopes	Whipped-cream substitute	1 envelope
1 cup	Milk	½ cup
1 tsp.	Vanilla	½ tsp.
About 2 cups	Blueberry-pie filling	About 1 cup

Bake pie shells according to package directions and allow to cool. Using an electric mixer, slowly blend softened cream cheese and sugar until smooth. Beat cream mix according to package directions, and fold it into cheese-sugar mixture. Add milk and vanilla and mix well. Fill pie shells and top cheese mixture with fruit, without stirring. Chill before serving.

COOK Henry E. Riley   CHIEF Jerry B. Black

Shrimp and
Eggplant Jambalaya

This fragrant and colorful Louisiana specialty is expertly prepared in a Baton Rouge firehouse kitchen.

SERVES 12	INGREDIENTS	SERVES 6
2	Eggplant	1
2 to 6 Tbs.	Cooking oil	2 to 3 Tbs.
1 cup	Onions	½ cup
1 cup	Celery	½ cup
1 cup	Green pepper	½ cup
2	Garlic cloves, crushed	1
2 No. 2 cans	Tomatoes	1 No. 2 can
2 cups	Rice	1 cup
To taste	Salt and pepper	To taste
As needed	Water	As needed
2 lbs.	Shrimp	1 lb.

Chop onions, celery, and green pepper and clean the shrimp. Peel and dice eggplant and sauté in cooking oil until tender. Add onions, celery, green pepper, and crushed garlic. Cook and stir about 5 minutes. Add chopped tomatoes and well-washed uncooked rice. Season with salt and pepper to taste and simmer for about 1 hour, adding shrimp during last 20 minutes of cooking time. Add water as needed from time to time to keep ingredients from sticking to the pan.

COOKS All personnel   CHIEF Edgar LeJeune

Chicken
in the Black Pot

SERVES 12	INGREDIENTS	SERVES 4
3 2½-lb. fryers	Chicken	1 2½-lb. fryer
To taste	Red pepper or paprika	To taste
To taste	Salt and pepper	To taste
About ½ cup	Flour	About ¼ cup
½ cup	Cooking oil	¼ cup
As needed	Water	As needed
¾ cup	Butter	¼ cup
2 Tbs.	Worcestershire sauce	2 tsp.
1½ lemons	Lemon juice	½ lemon
3	Garlic cloves	1
3 4-oz. cans	Mushrooms	1 4-oz. can

Gravy

3 pkgs.	Brown-gravy mix	1 pkg.
3 cups	Water	1 cup
To garnish	Parsley	To garnish

Quarter the chickens and season them with red pepper or paprika, salt, and pepper to taste. Pat lightly with flour. Heat cooking oil to cover the bottom of a large pot, and brown chicken on all sides. When chicken is browned, add water to a depth of about 1″ in the pot, and cook, covered, over low heat. Meanwhile combine lemon juice, garlic, butter, Worcestershire sauce, and the liquid from canned mushrooms in a bowl; add to the chicken and continue to cook. Baste the chicken with the cooking liquid once or twice during cooking time. When the chicken is done, take it out of the pot and set aside. Skim excess fat from pot and discard.

Add drained mushrooms and gravy mix with water and cook 5 minutes more. Just before serving, garnish with parsley.

Suggestion: The firehouse crew in Lafayette serves this chicken dish with peas, mashed potatoes, and a fruit salad.

COOK Larry Broussard   CHIEF P. J. Benoit

Shrimp Gumbo

SERVES 8	INGREDIENTS	SERVES 4
¾ cup	Corn oil margarine	6 Tbs.
3 lbs.	Shrimp	1½ lbs.
6 Tbs.	Flour	3 Tbs.
2 qts.	Water	1 qt.
2 6½-oz cans	Crab meat	1 6½-oz. can
2 4-oz. jars	Pimentoes, chopped	1 4-oz. jar
2 cups	Green onions	1 cup
2 small	Green pepper	1 small
2 tsp.	Garlic salt	1 tsp.
½ tsp.	Pepper	¼ tsp.
2 Tbs.	Worcestershire sauce	1 Tbs.
2 Tbs.	Paprika	1 Tbs.
2 8-oz. pkgs.	Okra, frozen	1 8-oz. pkg.
2 jars (1 pint)	Oysters	1 jar (½ pint)
2 Tbs.	Filé	1 Tbs.

Chop onions. In a skillet, melt margarine and steam the shrimp in it, stirring occasionally, till any water has evaporated. Add flour to skillet to make roux, and stir into shrimp. Add water, crab meat, pimentoes, onions, and all other ingredients but okra, oysters, and filé. Simmer on a medium fire for 45 mintues or 1 hour, stirring periodically. Add okra and oysters and cook 20 to 30 minutes more. Turn off the heat, let stand for a minute, and add filé.

Suggestion: Serve over rice, with a lettuce-and-tomato salad and cornbread.

COOK C. E. Fredieu   CHIEF Dallas W. Green, Jr.

Chicken
and Spaghetti

For a new way to serve both chicken and spaghetti, try combining the two by simmering cooked, boned chicken in a tomato sauce served over spaghetti and topped with Parmesan cheese.

SERVES 12	INGREDIENTS	SERVES 6
2 2½- to 3-lb. fryers	Chicken	1 2½- to 3-lb. fryer
As needed	Water	As needed
1 Tbs.	Salt	½ Tbs.
2	Onions	1
1	Green pepper	½
3 stalks	Celery	1½ stalks
3 cups	Chicken broth	1½ cups
3 15-oz. cans	Tomato sauce	1 15-oz. can
To taste	Salt and pepper	To taste
	Spaghetti	
	Parmesan cheese	

Cut chicken into pieces, cover with salted water, and cook until tender. Bone chicken and set aside. Chop onions, green peppers, and celery, and add to cooking water of chicken, along with additional broth. Add tomato sauce, salt, and pepper. Simmer for 1½ hours over low heat. While sauce is cooking, cut chicken in bite-size pieces and add to sauce. Prepare spaghetti according to package directions. Serve topped with sauce and grated Parmesan cheese.

COOK Alvin Polvick   CHIEF Musick

Kemp's
Mexican Dish

SERVES 12	INGREDIENTS	SERVES 6
6 lbs.	Ground beef	3 lbs.
1 No. 303 can	Jalapeña peppers and tomatoes	½ No. 303 can
2 No. 2 cans	Spanish rice	1 No. 2 can
½ No. 303 can	Enchilada sauce	¼ No. 303 can
12	Tortillas	6
2 small	Onions	1 small
4	Tomatoes	2
1 head	Lettuce	½ head
1 lb.	American cheese	½ lb.

In a large skillet, sauté meat and drain excess grease. Add the Jalapeña peppers and tomatoes, Spanish rice, and enchilada sauce to meat and simmer for about ½ hour. Fry tortillas until light brown. Chop onions, tomatoes, lettuce, and grate cheese. Stuff half of the meat mixture into folded tortillas to make tacos, and place them in a baking dish. Cover with remaining sauce, cheese, tomatoes, and onions (in this order) and heat in a 400° oven until cheese melts. Cover with crisp chopped lettuce and serve.

COOK Jimmy Kemp   CHIEF W. Hershel Sharp

Broccoli–Rice–Cheese

*A combination of cheese and condensed soup produces a
creamy sauce for a delicious rice and broccoli dish.*

SERVES 12	INGREDIENTS	SERVES 6
1 Tbs.	Shortening	½ Tbs.
1 small	Onion, chopped	½ small
½ cup	Celery, chopped	¼ cup
1 cup	Rice	½ cup
2 10-oz. pkgs.	Broccoli, frozen	1 10-oz. pkg.
1 10½-oz. can	Cream of mushroom soup	½ 10½-oz. can
1 10½-oz. can	Cream of chicken soup	½ 10½-oz. can
8-ozs.	Pasteurized cheese spread	4 ozs.
To taste	Salt and pepper	To taste

Sauté chopped onion and diced celery in shortening. Cook rice and
broccoli separately. Mix undiluted soup, cheese, and sautéed onions and celery together for sauce and season with salt and pepper.
Add the cooked rice to the sauce. Arrange drained broccoli in a
baking dish and pour the cheese-rice mixture over it. Bake for 10
to 20 minutes at 375°, or until cheese melts.

COOK Jimmy Kemp   CHIEF W. Hershel Sharp

Homemade Ice Cream

YIELDS TWO GALLONS	INGREDIENTS	YIELDS ONE GALLON
10	Eggs	5
3 cups	Sugar	1½ cups
1 qt.	Milk	1 pt.
1 qt.	Half-n-half	1 pt.
1 qt.	Whipping cream	1 pt.
1 jar	Marshmallow cream	½ jar
2 16-oz. pkgs.	Strawberries, frozen	1 16-oz. pkg.

Rock salt
Crushed ice

Beat eggs, sugar, and milk, and cook over low heat until mixture starts to boil and is thick enough to coat spoon. (Do not boil.) Remove from heat and let cool. Add half-n-half, whipped cream, marshmallow cream, and strawberries. Stir well. Add extra milk if needed so container will be three-quarters full of mixture. Place container in the freezer tub, and add crushed ice and rock salt, allowing 8 parts ice to 1 part rock salt. After ice cream is frozen, you may want it to become even firmer. If so, remove dasher, replace cover of container, drain brine from tub, and repack with ice and salt. Cover with paper and let stand at least 30 minutes.

COOKS Tiny and Robert Stokes   CHIEF W. Hershel Sharp

Tulsa Chili

Firefighters in every part of the country love chili. This version is more beefy, with less tomato sauce. The firemen in Tulsa sometimes serve it over spaghetti.

SERVES 8	INGREDIENTS	SERVES 4
2 lbs.	Ground beef	1 lb.
1 medium	Onion, chopped	1 small
A few Tbs.	Shortening	1 or 2 Tbs.
2 Tbs.	Chili powder	1 Tbs.
1 tsp.	Cumin	½ tsp.
2 tsp.	Salt	1 tsp.
2	Garlic cloves, crushed	1
2 10½-oz. cans	Beef broth	1 10½-oz. can
1 8-oz. can	Tomato sauce	½ 8-oz. can
2 cups	Pinto beans, canned	1 cup
A few Tbs.	Flour	1 or 2 Tbs.

Brown the meat and chopped onions in shortening, and pour off excess fat. Add chili powder, cumin, salt, crushed garlic, broth, and tomato sauce. Cover and simmer for 45 minutes. Add pinto beans and simmer 15 minutes more. Thicken with a small amount of flour paste (1 tablespoon flour to ¼ cup water). Serve as a sauce over cooked spaghetti or plain with saltines.

COOK L. R. Schmidt   CHIEF E. Stanley Hawkins

Beef Burgundy

This easy-to-prepare dish is delicious served with potatoes,
noodles, or rice. Or try serving the gravy over hot biscuits.

SERVES 12	INGREDIENTS	SERVES 6
4 to 4½ lbs.	Stew beef	2 to 2½ lbs.
4 cans	Cream of mushroom or golden mushroom soup	2 cans
1½ cups	Burgundy wine	¾ cup

Combine the soup with wine and pour over beef in a large pan.
Cover and bake in a 350° oven for 2½ hours. (Beef may be
browned first in skillet, using a little shortening.) If gravy seems
to need additional liquid after the first hour, add a little water.

Note: Cooking sherry may be substituted for Burgundy wine.

cooks All personnel   chief E. Stanley Hawkins

German Casserole

SERVES 12	INGREDIENTS	SERVES 6
12	Pork chops	6
To taste	Salt and pepper	To taste
4 Tbs.	Shortening	2 Tbs.
8	Potatoes	4
2 No. 303 cans	Sauerkraut	1 No. 303 can
¼ cup	Water	A few Tbs.

Season the chops and brown in a skillet in heated shortening. Place chops in the bottom of casserole baking dish. Slice or dice potatoes, place them on top of chops, and season with salt and pepper. Mound sauerkraut on top of potatoes. Remove excess fat from skillet used to brown chops, add a little water, and heat. Pour the resulting brown broth over sauerkraut. Cover casserole and bake in a 325° oven for 2 to 2½ hours.

COOKS All personnel   CHIEF E. Stanley Hawkins

Kraut Piccalilli

Here is an easy-to-prepare relish that can be stored for several weeks in the refrigerator. It's good served with cooked beans, black-eyed peas and pork, or as a relish for hot dogs and hamburgers.

YIELDS ABOUT 1½ QUARTS	INGREDIENTS	YIELDS ABOUT 1½ PINTS
2 No. 303 cans	Sauerkraut, chopped	1 No. 303 can
2 cups	Celery, chopped	1 cup
½ cup	Onion, chopped	¼ cup
¼ cup	Green pepper, chopped	⅛ cup
¼ cup	Pimentoes, chopped	⅛ cup
⅔ cup	Vinegar	⅓ cup
2 cups	Sugar	1 cup

In a mixing bowl, combine the sauerkraut, celery, onion, green pepper, and pimentoes. Boil the vinegar and sugar together in a saucepan until syrupy. Pour this syrup over sauerkraut mixture. Let cool, then refrigerate.

COOK William L. Howell   CHIEF E. Stanley Hawkins

Bite-Size
Corn Dogs

This recipe, sent to us by Allen Hartshorn of the Texarkana fire department, uses an onion ring batter that can also be used for deep frying shimp or other seafood.

SERVES 8	INGREDIENTS	SERVES 4
1 cup	Corn meal mix	½ cup
1 cup	Flour	½ cup
½ tsp.	Salt	¼ tsp.
1 Tbs.	Baking powder	½ Tbs.
1 Tbs.	Sugar	½ Tbs.
1 tsp.	Onion salt	½ tsp.
½ tsp.	Garlic salt	¼ tsp.
1 cup	Milk	½ cup
2	Eggs	1
1 pkg.	Frankfurters	½ pkg.
For deep frying	Cooking oil	For deep frying

Cut the frankfurters into bite-size pieces. Mix all batter ingredients together and stir well. Dip the frankfurter pieces into the batter, letting excess drain off. Drop pieces into deep, hot fat and fry until golden brown. Drain well on paper towels before serving.

COOKS All personnel   CHIEF Gene Davis

Chocolate Pie

YIELDS FOUR 9″ PIES	INGREDIENTS	YIELDS ONE 9″ PIE
	Filling	
4 cups	Sugar	1 cup
1 cup	Flour	¼ cup
¾ cup	Cocoa	3 heaping Tbs.
8 cups	Milk	2 cups
8	Egg yolks	2
½ cup	Margarine	2 Tbs.
½ tsp.	Salt	⅛ tsp.
1 Tbs.	Vanilla	1 tsp.
4 9″ shells	Pie pastry, frozen	1 9″ shell
	Meringue	
8	Egg whites	2
1 cup	Sugar	¼ cup

Mix the sugar, flour, and cocoa together in a saucepan, gradually blending in milk. Place on medium heat until lukewarm. Separate eggs (reserving whites for meringue). Blend a small amount of warm sauce from pan into egg yolks, and then add the mixture to the pan. Add margarine, and continue cooking over medium heat, stirring often until mixture thickens to the consistency of mayonnaise. Remove from heat, add salt and vanilla, and cool. Bake pie crusts and cool before pouring chocolate filling into them.

Meringue: Beat egg whites, add sugar, and continue beating until peaks form. Mound on pie. Place under broiler at 350° and brown lightly. Cool and serve.

Suggestion: For a variation, top the pie with whipped cream instead of meringue.

COOK Ralph Murdaugh   CHIEF Ben Warlick

Spanish
Bean Soup

SERVES 12 TO 14	INGREDIENTS	SERVES 6 TO 8
1⅓ cups	Navy beans	⅔ cup
1⅓ cups	Northern beans	⅔ cup
4 qts.	Water	2 qts.
4 tsp.	Salt	2 tsp.
4 Tbs.	Green pepper	2 Tbs.
½ cup	Onion	¼ cup
4 Tbs.	Celery	2 Tbs.
½ tsp.	Cumin	¼ tsp.
1 Tbs.	Chili powder	½ Tbs.
½ tsp.	Cayenne pepper	A pinch or two
1 cup	Tomatoes, drained	½ cup
1 Tbs.	Baco chips	½ Tbs.

Prepare beans for cooking according to package directions. (Some dried beans require pre-soaking, others do not.) Pick over beans, and add to boiling salted water. Chop the green pepper, onion, and celery. Reduce heat to medium and add all remaining ingredients except baco chips. When tomatoes are cooked down, add baco chips and simmer until all ingredients are done. Add hot water to make soup thinner or mash some of the beans and return to soup for last 15 minutes of cooking time to thicken.

COOKS All personnel   CHIEF Frank J. Quinn

One-Pound-Can
Bread

Round, golden loaves of bread are served fresh from the oven here, and buttered while still warm. Since there is a knack to baking bread this way, practice may be required to perfect this recipe. It's worth the effort.

YIELDS TWO LOAVES	INGREDIENTS	YIELDS ONE LOAF
1 cup	Milk	½ cup
1 pkg.	Yeast	½ pkg.
2 Tbs.	Sugar	1 Tbs.
2 tsp.	Salt	1 tsp.
About 4 cups	Flour	About 2 cups
¼ cup	Liquid cooking oil	⅛ cup
2	Eggs	1
2 1-lb. cans	Coffee cans	1 1-lb. can

Heat milk to lukewarm, and dissolve yeast in it. Add sugar and salt and stir until dissolved. Put half the flour in a bowl and blend in milk-yeast mixture. Mix in the cooking oil and eggs. Add just enough additional flour to keep dough from being sticky. Turn onto floured board and knead until dough is elastic but light, or about 10 minutes. Press the dough into a greased coffee can so that it is ⅓ to ½ full. Cover with the lid or with aluminum foil and set in a warm place to rise for about 1 hour until dough fills can. Remove the lid and bake in the can at 375° for 20 to 25 minutes. Let stand a few minutes. Remove bread from can, butter, and serve while warm.

COOK Bob Gregory   CHIEF Earl R. McDaniel

*About
Systems
of
Firehouse
Cooking*

Systems of meal preparation in today's fire departments are designed to suit the particular needs and schedules of the men and women at each station. They adopt cooking and eating habits they like best. Because their job requires around-the-clock hours, most firefighters eat at least one or two meals in the firehouse kitchen.

Generally the firefighters at all stations take turns with the kitchen duties. Many stations have an elected cooking crew with a clean-up crew to put things back in order. Each shift at each station has a cook, however. In Lubbock, Texas there are eleven stations with three shifts at each station and a cook for each shift, making 33 cooks. In Milwaukee, Wisconsin, there are 33 stations, with three shifts—99 cooks!

Menus are often determined by the season or the availability of certain foods. Many off-duty firefighters like to hunt and fish. If the catch is good, they may bring fresh fish or game—deer, wild goose, or rabbit—to the station. In Idaho Falls, Idaho, the men go on company hunts of eight to ten and have no trouble finding someone to donate hunting tags to the fire department. They have their own butcher shop in the basement of the fire department, complete with wrapping table, cutting block, meat cuber, and hamburger grinder.

In other cities and towns, vegetables are grown in a small garden patch beside a station. Some volunteers who have farms bring in generous supplies of fresh vegetables and fruits, or dairy and poultry products to add to the firehouse larder.

At each station men are elected to buy groceries and replenish the staples kept on hand in the firehouse kitchen. The rule is that each man who eats at the firehouse contributes equally to the cost of the food. The amount is usually nominal, averaging one to two dollars a day for each man. So these meals are really a bargain, and well worth the time and money spent in grocery shopping, cooking, and cleaning up.

from the
Mountain and Pacific States,
Alaska, and Hawaii

ALASKA

HAWAII

A Meat Loaf
from Montana

The men here prepare dinner and supper each day at the
station. The recipe below is for one of the most popular dishes
in all firehouse kitchens—meat loaf.

SERVES 8 TO 10	INGREDIENTS	SERVES 4 TO 6
3 lbs.	Ground beef	1½ lbs.
2	Onions, chopped	1
1 Tbs.	Salt	1½ tsp.
To taste	Pepper	To taste
1 14½-oz. can	Stewed tomatoes	About 1 cup
About 1 cup	Cracker crumbs	About ½ cup
4 to 6 Tbs.	Catsup	2 to 3 Tbs.

In a large bowl mix ground beef with chopped onions. Add salt, pepper, stewed tomatoes and cracker crumbs. Place in greased baking pan or dish, and shape into loaf. Spread catsup on top of meat loaf and bake for 1½ to 2 hours in a 350° oven.

COOKS All personnel   CHIEF Herbert Hoey

Sour-Cream
Enchiladas

Cooking skills are easily acquired in this department. Some say self-defense is the reason that wives often suggest home-tested recipes.

SERVES 6 TO 8	INGREDIENTS	SERVES 4 TO 5
1 cup	Green onions	½ cup
2 cups	Sour cream	1 cup
½ tsp.	Cumin	¼ tsp.
4 cups	Cheddar cheese	2 cups
12	Tortillas	6
2 to 4 Tbs.	Cooking oil	1 to 2 Tbs.
10 ozs.	Enchilada sauce	5 ozs.

Chop onions and grate cheese. Combine the onions, sour cream, cumin, and about a quarter of the cheese. Fry tortillas in a small amount of oil and dip into heated enchilada sauce. Spread about 5 tablespoons of the sour cream mixture over the center of each tortilla and roll. Place tortilla rolls side by side in an ungreased casserole dish. Spread remaining cheese evenly over the top. Bake, uncovered, in a 375° oven for 20 minutes, and garnish with any remaining sour-cream-onion mixture before serving.

COOKS Don Campbell and Reg Christman   CHIEF B. J. McCarrell

Aurora
Steak Roll

A footnote to this recipe stated, "The gravy is great over mashed or baked potatoes." It's great over piping hot biscuits, too.

YIELDS TWO STEAK ROLLS TO SERVE 8	INGREDIENTS	YIELDS ONE STEAK ROLL TO SERVE 4
2 1½-lb. slices	Top round or flank steak	1 1½-lb. slice
3 Tbs.	Prepared mustard	4 tsp.
To taste	Salt and pepper	To taste
1 cut lengthwise	Carrot	½ cut lengthwise
2	Kosher-style dill pickles	1
2 cups	Flour	1 cup
½ cup	Shortening	¼ cup
4 cups	Water	2 cups
1½ to 2 cups	Sour cream	¾ to 1 cup

Lay slices of steak out flat and pound lightly. Spread each slice with mustard, and season lightly with salt and pepper. Place half of a carrot, cut lengthwise, on each steak along with a slice of dill pickle. Roll steak, and tie securely, wrapping string around steak in several places crosswise and also lengthwise. Flour steak rolls well, heat shortening in deep skillet or heavy pan, and brown on all sides, turning often. Add water and reduce heat. Cover and simmer for 1 to 1½ hours, or until steak is tender. Remove steak rolls to serving dish. Slowly stir sour cream into pan juices and simmer for several minutes. Remove strings from steak roll and slice into serving pieces.

COOKS All personnel   CHIEF William H. Hawkins

Chicken Casserole
with Cashews

SERVES 8 TO 10	INGREDIENTS	SERVES 4 TO 6
2 fryers	Chicken	1 fryer
½ cup	Cooking oil	¼ cup
2 cups	Water or chicken broth	1 cup
1 cup	Onions, chopped	½ cup
2 cups	Cashews	1 cup
4 cups	Celery, chopped	2 cups
To taste	Salt and pepper	To taste
4 cans	Cream of mushroom soup	2 cans
4 3-oz. cans	Chow-mein noodles	2 3-oz. cans

Cut up chicken and fry in oil until browned and tender. When it is cool, bone and dice meat. Combine chicken with all other ingredients except noodles. Place noodles in greased casserole dish, and spread the chicken mixture over noodles. Bake in a 350° oven for about 20 minutes.

COOK George Karns   CHIEF Argus Cummings

Fudge Brownies

A cookbook representing the favorite foods of so many American men was certain to include a recipe for brownies.

YIELDS TWO 8″ PANS	INGREDIENTS	YIELDS ONE 8″ PAN
1 cup	Margarine	½ cup
4 squares	Unsweetened chocolate	2 squares
1½ cups	Flour	¾ cup
½ tsp.	Baking powder	¼ tsp.
1 tsp.	Salt	½ tsp.
2 cups	Sugar	1 cup
4	Eggs	2
2 tsp.	Vanilla	1 tsp.
1 cup	Walnuts or pecans, chopped	½ cup

Melt margarine and chocolate together in double boiler and let cool. Sift together flour, baking powder, and salt and set aside. In a large mixing bowl, add sugar to eggs and mix thoroughly. Add vanilla, cooled chocolate mixture, dry ingredients, and chopped nuts. Pour batter into greased 8″ baking pans. Bake at 350° for approximately 20 to 25 minutes.

Note: Frosting recipe follows.

COOK George Karns   CHIEF Argus Cummings

Fudge Frosting

ICES TWO LAYERS	INGREDIENTS	ICES ONE LAYER
2 squares	Unsweetened chocolate	1 square
3 Tbs.	Butter	1½ Tbs.
5 Tbs.	Milk	2½ Tbs.
¼ tsp.	Salt	A pinch
1 tsp.	Vanilla	½ tsp.
2 cups	Confectioners' sugar	1 cup

Combine chocolate, butter, and milk in a double boiler. Add salt and vanilla. Remove from heat, stir in enough confectioners' sugar to make mixture of spreading consistency, and smooth over brownies or cake.

COOK George Karns   CHIEF Argus Cummings

Chop Suey

The Denver fire department is justly proud of its cooks. Some have had professional experience, others have taken gourmet courses, and many have just inherited their talent from a long line of good family cooks.

SERVES 10	INGREDIENTS	SERVES 5
2½ lbs.	Stew beef	1¼ lbs.
2½ lbs.	Pork shoulder	1¼ lbs.
1 large stalk	Celery	1 small stalk
1 large	Onion	1 small
4 Tbs.	Cooking oil	2 Tbs.
4 Tbs.	Soy sauce	2 Tbs.
To taste	Salt	To taste
As needed	Water	As needed
2 No. 2½ cans	Bean sprouts	1 No. 2½ can
1 8-oz. can	Bamboo shoots	4 ozs.
1 8-oz. can	Sliced water chestnuts	4 ozs.
12 to 15	Fresh mushrooms	6 to 8
	Brown-gravy beads (optional)	
About 2 Tbs.	Cornstarch	About 1 Tbs.

Rice or
chow-mein noodles

Cube beef and pork into 1″ pieces, cut celery in ½″ slices crosswise, and dice onion. Brown meat, celery, and onion in heated cooking oil. Mix in soy sauce while browning and sprinkle with salt. Add water to cover ingredients and simmer 1 hour. Drain and add bean sprouts, bamboo shoots, and water chestnuts. Slice and add the mushrooms, and simmer for 1 additional hour. For darker broth, add a small amount of brown-gravy beads. Five minutes before serving add cornstarch dissolved in water to thicken. Serve over fluffy cooked rice or with chow-mein noodles.

COOK Robert Dieckman   CHIEF Myrle K. Wise

Zucchini Stew

A good cook in the Denver firehouse kitchen is highly regarded and no one steps on his toes—although verbal abuse may be tolerated. When guests are invited to lunch at the firehouse they usually leave full and very impressed.

SERVES 12	INGREDIENTS	SERVES 6
12 small or 8 medium	Zucchini squash	6 small or 4 medium
2	White onions	1
4 small cloves	Garlic	2 small cloves
¼ cup	Olive oil	⅛ cup
2 No. 2½ cans	Tomatoes	1 No. 2½ can
6 cups	Water	3 cups
To taste	Salt and pepper	To taste
1 tsp.	Basil	½ tsp.
¼ tsp.	Oregano	A pinch
2 Tbs.	Parsley	1 Tbs.
½ cup	Romano cheese	¼ cup
8 large	Potatoes	4 large

Cut squash in slices about 1″ thick, slice onion and mince garlic. Heat oil in a large pan or pot. Over low heat sauté squash, onion, and garlic in oil. When squash is lightly browned, add tomatoes (hand squeeze before adding to remove juice.) Add water, seasonings, and Romano cheese. Quarter potatoes and add to stew. Cook, covered, over low heat for approximately 1 hour, or until fork will penetrate potatoes easily. Pan lid should be left slightly open during cooking time, but add water if broth becomes too thick.

COOK Herman Monaco   CHIEF Myrle K. Wise

Shrimp Creole

SERVES 8	INGREDIENTS	SERVES 4
1 cup	Onions	½ cup
1 cup	Celery	½ cup
¼ tsp.	Garlic	⅛ tsp.
6 Tbs.	Cooking oil	3 Tbs.
2 large	Tomatoes	1 large
2 8-oz. cans	Tomato sauce	1 8-oz. can
1 tsp.	Salt	½ tsp.
2 tsp.	Sugar	1 tsp.
2 tsp.	Chili powder	1 tsp.
2 Tbs.	Worcestershire sauce	1 Tbs.
2 dashes	Hot red-pepper sauce	1 dash
4 tsp.	Cornstarch	2 tsp.
1½ lbs.	Shrimp	¾ lb.
1 cup	Green pepper, chopped	½ cup

Chop onions, celery and garlic and cook them in hot oil until tender, but not brown. Add sliced tomatoes, tomato sauce, and seasonings. Simmer, uncovered, for about 45 minutes. Dissolve cornstarch in a little water and stir this paste into sauce. Cook, stirring, until mixture thickens and bubbles. Add shrimp and green peppers. Cover and simmer about 20 minutes. Serve over rice.

COOKS All personnel   CHIEF Bruce Forbes

Boshears Chops

*After a special meeting to pick a favorite recipe, the firefighters
in Farmington chose this recipe.*

SERVES 8	INGREDIENTS	SERVES 4
8	Pork chops	4
To taste	Salt and pepper	To taste
To taste	Garlic salt	To taste
2	Eggs	1
⅔ cup	Milk	⅓ cup
2 cups	Bread crumbs	1 cup
3 Tbs.	Cooking oil	1½ Tbs.
About 2 tsp.	Brown sugar	About 1 tsp.
Several dashes	Worcestershire sauce	Dash or two
2	Lemons	1
2 8-oz. cans	Tomato sauce	1 8-oz. can

Season pork chops with salt, pepper, and garlic salt. Beat eggs
and milk together. Dip chops in this mixture, then coat each one
well with bread crumbs. Brown chops on both sides in heated
cooking oil on top of the stove, about 3 minutes on each side.
Sprinkle brown sugar and a few drops of Worcestershire sauce on
each chop. Slice lemons, and lay the slices on the chops. Pour
tomato sauce over all. Cook for 15 minutes on top of stove. Bake,
uncovered, in a 375° oven for 30 minutes, turning once.

Suggestion: Serve with spaghetti and garlic bread.

COOK Walt Boshears   CHIEF William E. McFarland

Dinner Rolls

All engineers and hosemen share cooking duties at this fire department, but the most famous chef is Dillis DeWitt. He is best known for his carrot cakes and dinner rolls. Most of the time spent preparing these rolls is in the waiting (not the working) and they're well worth it.

YIELDS TWO DOZEN	INGREDIENTS	YIELDS ONE DOZEN
2 pkg.	Yeast	1 pkg.
1 cup	Water	½ cup
1 cup	Milk	½ cup
1	Egg, beaten	1
2 tsp.	Salt	1 tsp.
¼ cup	Sugar	⅛ cup
About 8 cups	Flour	About 4 cups
4 Tbs.	Margarine, melted	2 Tbs.

In separate pans, warm the water and the milk. In a mixing bowl, add the yeast to the lukewarm water. Mix warm milk, beaten egg, salt, and sugar into yeast mixture. Add about half of the flour and mix. Stir in melted margarine and continue adding flour until dough is no longer sticky. Knead on floured board until dough is elastic but not dry. Place in a greased bowl and turn over once. Cover and keep in a warm place until dough doubles in size, or about 1 hour. Turn onto floured board, press down to ½″ thickness to remove air bubbles, and shape into rolls. Let rise again until double (about 45 minutes). Bake in a preheated 350° oven about 15 minutes, or until browned.

COOK Dillis DeWitt   CHIEF Hugh D. Hutchinson

Meat Loaf
with a Twist

The main ingredients in this recipe—beef, macroni, and cheese —are proven firehouse favorites. Here they are combined in a flavorful, economical dish.

SERVES 12 TO 14	INGREDIENTS	SERVES 6 TO 8
4 cups	Twist macaroni	2 cups
2	Onions	1
1 large	Green pepper	1 small
1 lb.	Swiss cheese	½ lb.
1 lb.	Cheddar cheese	½ lb.
2 lbs.	Ground beef	1 lb.
1 large	Egg	1 medium
1 4-oz. can	Mushrooms	About 2 ozs.
½ tsp.	Oregano	¼ tsp.
½ tsp.	Garlic salt	¼ tsp.
To taste	Salt and pepper	To taste
1 cup	Tomato sauce	½ cup

Boil twist macaroni for only 6 to 7 minutes, drain and set aside. Chop onions and green pepper. Cut swiss cheese and cheddar cheese into ½″ squares. Add chopped ingredients and macaroni to ground beef along with egg and sliced mushrooms, with juice from the can. Add all seasonings and mix well. Form into a loaf and place in greased baking dish. Pour tomato sauce over the loaf and bake 1 to 1½ hours at 400° until meat loaf is done.

COOK Robert Nielsen   CHIEF Leon R. DeKorver

Captain Farnsworth's Recipe from
Old Mexico (Green Chilies with Tortillas)

The heat of the beef-chili mixture for this recipe is determined by the number of chili peppers used. Red chilies will produce a much hotter dish and may be substituted for green chilies. Firefighters just might prefer the less mild version!

SERVES 8 TO 10	INGREDIENTS	SERVES 4 TO 6
4 lbs.	Ground beef	2 lbs.
4 Tbs.	Cooking oil	2 Tbs.
As needed	Water	As needed
2 4-oz. cans	Green chili peppers	1 4-oz. can
4 to 8	Yellow chili peppers	2 to 4
2 10-oz. pkgs.	Sharp cheddar cheese	1 10-oz. pkg.
15	Tortillas	7
	Butter	

Cook meat in heated oil until well done. Chop beef into small bits while frying. When meat is done, drain off all liquid and grease. Spread the dry meat evenly in the bottom of a frying pan, and add water to cover. Combine chili peppers well with meat, and level off mixture again. Grate cheese and spread evenly over the meat mixture. Do not stir mixture after cheese is added. Simmer about 30 minutes, or until cheese is completely melted, then stir cheese into meat mixture. Serve warm with flour tortillas.

Note: Flour tortillas may be fried while cheese is melting. Butter both sides of flour tortillas and cook in dry skillet until brown spots appear, about 30 seconds. Fry both sides. Ready-made tortillas are available frozen or canned in supermarkets.

COOK John A. Farnsworth   CHIEF W. D. Richard

Cabbage Rolls

The chef responsible for this dish is Czechoslovakian and the recipe was given to him by his family. It was a first-prize winner in a local cooking contest in Boise.

SERVES 10 TO 12	INGREDIENTS	SERVES 6 TO 8
1 large head	Cabbage	1 medium head
1 medium	Onion	1 small
2 Tbs.	Butter	1 Tbs.
3 lbs.	Ground beef	1½ lbs.
1 cup	Rice, cooked	½ cup
2	Eggs	1
¼ tsp.	Celery salt	⅛ tsp.
To taste	Salt and pepper	To taste
2 No. 303 cans	Sauerkraut	1 No. 303 can
4 10½-oz. cans	Tomato soup	2 10½-oz. cans
To dilute soup	Water	To dilute soup

Use cabbage that is not too firm. Remove core with a sharp knife and scald in boiling salted water. Remove a few leaves at a time, and trim the thick ridge from back of leaves to make it easier for rolling. Chop the small leaves to use later on top of finished cabbage rolls. Sauté onion in butter until transparent. Combine the onion with the meat, rice, egg, and seasonings, and mix well. Spread the thick end of each leaf with this filling to about ¾" thickness, fold the opposite sides and roll, starting with the thick end. Fasten with toothpicks. Place rolls in a buttered baking dish and cover with reserved chopped leaves. Top with sauerkraut and diluted tomato soup. Bake, covered, at 325° for about 2 hours, or until browned and tender.

COOK John Boros   CHIEF David F. Perry

Tacos

---

*Tacos are a Mexican favorite which first won popularity in the
southwestern United States, then became a northwestern
favorite, as in Yakima, and are now prepared nationwide. They
may be filled with a variety of ingredients. The trick is to heap
and eat the taco without allowing the ingredients to escape
your grasp.*

YIELDS TWO DOZEN TO SERVE 8 TO 10	INGREDIENTS	YIELDS ONE DOZEN TO SERVE 4 TO 6
2 lbs.	Ground beef	1 lb.
1 large	Onion	1 small
1 tsp.	Salt	½ tsp.
1 tsp.	Oregano	½ tsp.
8 Tbs.	Tomato paste or catsup	4 Tbs.
24	Tortillas	12
2 cups or more	Cooking oil	1 cup or more
1 head	Lettuce, chopped	½ head
	Tomato juice, taco sauce, or fresh tomatoes	
2 cups	Cheddar cheese, grated	1 cup

Chop the onion and brown it with the meat in a frying pan. Add
salt, oregano, tomato paste or catsup, and cook until meat and
onions are done. In a separate pan, fry the tortillas, one at a time,
in a small amount of heated cooking oil (about three tablespoons
apiece) for a few seconds until they are softened. Remove tortillas
from pan and drain. Put one heaping tablespoon of meat mixture
on each tortilla and fold. Secure with toothpick if necessary. Add
additional shortening to pan and fry each tortilla until it is crisp.

(If a softer taco is preferred, do not refry tortilla.) Garnish each taco with finely chopped lettuce and either a teaspoon or two of tomato juice or taco sauce, or chopped fresh tomatoes. Season with salt, sprinkle with grated cheese, and serve warm.

cooks All personnel   chief Matson A. Young

Broiled Salmon

The Rogue River is within five miles of one of the fire stations in Medford. This river is well known to connoisseurs of rainbow trout or steelhead, Chinook and silver salmon. Here is an easy way to prepare the fish.

SERVES 12	INGREDIENTS	SERVES 6
12	Salmon steaks	6
½ cup	Butter, melted	¼ cup
To taste	Salt and pepper	To taste
To taste	Lemon juice or seafood sauce	To taste

Brush fish with melted butter, and season with salt and pepper. Broil for about 10 minutes, then turn steaks. Brush with butter, season, and broil for 10 additional minutes, or until done. Serve with lemon juice or seafood sauce.

COOK Kenneth Struck   CHIEF Eugene P. Robertson

Huckleberry
Upside-Down Cake

Huckleberries are plentiful in the high elevations of Oregon and Washington. They are hard to pick and sell for a good price—if a prospective buyer can find someone willing to sell his berries after working so hard to pick them.

YIELDS TWO 9" CAKES	INGREDIENTS	YIELDS ONE 9" CAKE
8 cups	Huckleberries (strawberries, blackberries, boysenberries, elderberries or blueberries)	4 cups
2 cups	Sugar	1 cup
	Batter	
3½ cups	Flour	1¾ cups
4 tsp.	Baking powder	2 tsp.
¼ tsp.	Salt	⅛ tsp.
1 cup	Shortening	½ cup
2 cups	Sugar	1 cup
4	Eggs	2
1 cup	Milk	½ cup
⅔ tsp.	Almond extract or vanilla	⅓ tsp.

Cook huckleberries with sugar for 10 minutes or until soft, and pour into a greased cake pan or iron skillet. Sift together the flour, baking powder, and salt and set aside. Cream shortening with sugar until fluffy. Add eggs and beat thoroughly. Stir in small amounts of sifted dry ingredients and milk alternately, beating well after each addition. Flavor with almond extract or vanilla. Pour batter over berry mixture and bake at 350° for 40 to 50 minutes. Loosen cake from sides with a spatula and turn out onto serving plate.

Suggestion: Serve topped with whipped cream or ice cream.

Firehouse
Clam Fritters

SERVES 12	INGREDIENTS	SERVES 6
12	Eggs	6
6 cups	Clams and juice	3 cups
1	Green pepper	½
1 medium	Onion	1 small
4 tsp.	Worcestershire or soy sauce	2 tsp.
Enough to thicken batter	Rice Krispies or corn flakes	Enough to thicken batter
As needed	Cooking oil	As needed

Beat eggs well with a fork. Chop the onion and pepper and combine with the eggs, clams and juice, and the Worcestershire or soy sauce. Crumble cereal and add until mixture thickens and is heavy enough to form into patties. Fry in hot cooking oil ½" to ¾" deep in frying pan.

Suggestion: Serve with white sauce, white onion gravy or tartar sauce and a tossed salad.

COOK Richard L. Barker   CHIEF Virgil V. Nave

Salmon Loaf

SERVES 8 TO 10	INGREDIENTS	SERVES 4 TO 6
2 1-lb. cans	Salmon	1 1-lb. can
1 cup	Liquid from salmon, plus milk	1/2 cup
2	Eggs	1
3 cups	Bread crumbs	1-1/2 cups
4 tsp.	Lemon juice	2 tsp.
2 small	Onions, chopped	1 small
1/2 tsp.	Salt	1/4 tsp.
1/4 tsp.	Pepper	1/8 tsp.
2 tsp.	Margarine or butter	1 tsp.
1/2 tsp.	Paprika	1/4 tsp.

Drain liquid from salmon into measuring cup, and combine with milk. After removing bones and skin, flake the salmon. Beat eggs together with fish. Add the salmon liquid and milk, bread crumbs, lemon juice, onions, and salt and pepper. Mold into shape in a greased loaf pan. Dot with butter or margarine and sprinkle with paprika. Bake in 350° oven for 30 to 40 minutes, or until brown and firm. Serve with lemon wedges.

COOKS Fire Department Auxiliary   CHIEF James Riley

Squash au Gratin

SERVES 8 TO 10	INGREDIENTS	SERVES 4 TO 6
6	Yellow squash	3
½ cup	Water	¼ cup
2 tsp.	Salt	1 tsp.
To taste	Pepper	To taste
1 large	Onion	1 small
2 slices	White bread	1 slice
4 Tbs.	Butter or margarine	2 Tbs.
1 cup	Cheddar cheese	½ cup

Cut the squash into ¼" slices. Chop onion and grate cheese. Place squash in a saucepan with water, salt, pepper, and onions. Cover and cook until tender, stirring occasionally. While squash is cooking, cut bread into small cubes and sauté in butter in frying pan until crisp. Spoon cooked squash and onion into heated serving dish. Sprinkle with grated cheese and toasted bread crumbs before serving.

COOKS Fire Department Auxiliary   CHIEF James Riley

Cranberry Salad

SERVES 15	INGREDIENTS	SERVES 5
1 1-lb. can	Cranberry sauce	⅓ 1-lb. can
3 3-oz. pkg.	Raspberry gelatin	1 3-oz. pkg.
3 cups	Water	1 cup
1½ cups	Apples	½ cup
1½ cups	Celery	½ cup
1½ cups	Crushed pineapple	½ cup
1½ cups	Pecans	½ cup

In a mixing bowl, combine cranberry sauce with dry gelatin and mash with a fork. Add hot water and stir until both cranberry sauce and gelatin are dissolved. Cool, then refrigerate until syrupy. Meanwhile, dice apples and chop celery. When partially set, remove from refrigerator and add apples, pineapple (with juice), celery, and nuts. Return to refrigerator until set and ready to serve.

Snickerdoodles

*A food dictionary defines "snickerdoodles" as "cookies rolled in
a mixture of cinnamon and sugar."*

YIELDS FOUR DOZEN	INGREDIENTS	YIELDS TWO DOZEN
1 cup	Margarine	½ cup
1½ cups	Sugar	¾ cup
2	Eggs	1
2½ cups	Flour	1¼ cups
1 tsp.	Baking soda	½ tsp.
2 tsp.	Cream of tartar	1 tsp.
¼ tsp.	Salt	⅛ tsp.
4 tsp.	Cinnamon	2 tsp.
5 Tbs.	Sugar	3 Tbs.

Soften and beat margarine until fluffy. Gradually add sugar. Beat
in eggs. Sift next four dry ingredients together and add slowly to
first mixture. Shape into walnut-size balls, role in mixture of
cinnamon and sugar, and place 2″ apart on an ungreased cookie
sheet. Bake in a 350° oven 12 to 15 minutes, or until light brown.
Cookies will flatten out to about 3″ in diameter as they bake. Let
cool on cookie sheet 3 to 5 minutes before removing to a rack to
finish cooling.

COOKS Fire Department Auxiliary   CHIEF James Riley

Apple Crisp from Anaheim

YIELDS TWO 6″ X 10″ PANS	INGREDIENTS	YIELDS ONE 6″ X 10″ PAN
1 cup	Butter or margarine	½ cup
10	Cooking apples	5
2 cups	Flour	1 cup
2 cups	Sugar	1 cup
1 tsp.	Baking powder	½ tsp.
1½ tsp.	Salt	¾ tsp.
1 tsp.	Cinnamon	½ tsp.
2	Eggs	1
4 Tbs.	Water	2 Tbs.
1 tsp.	Vanilla	½ tsp.
	Additional cinnamon	

Melt butter or margarine, and set aside to cool. Cut pared apples into thin slices and spread over bottom of greased 6″ x 10″ pans. Combine the flour, sugar, baking powder, salt, and cinnamon. Add unbeaten eggs to dry ingredients and stir until mixture is crumbly. Spread evenly over the sliced apples. Combine water and vanilla in a cup and spoon evenly over top of dish. Drizzle cooled, melted butter or margarine over all, sprinkle with additional cinnamon, and bake 30 to 40 minutes at 350°. Serve warm or cool, with cream or plain.

COOKS Fire Department Auxiliary   CHIEF James Riley

Chili
Casserole

The peppery taste of this dish can be varied with the number of chilies used—more or less according to your taste.

SERVES 6 TO 8	INGREDIENTS	SERVES 3 TO 4
2 4-oz. cans	Green chilies	1 4-oz. can
2	Eggs	1
3 cups	Milk	1½ cups
1 cup	Biscuit mix	½ cup
1 lb.	Sharp cheddar cheese	½ lb.
2 10-oz. cans	enchilada sauce	1 10-oz. can

Drain and split chilies, and place them in the bottom of a buttered casserole dish or baking pan. In a bowl beat eggs thoroughly. Grate the cheese and add to the beaten eggs along with the biscuit mix and milk. Pour over the chilies and bake in a 325° oven for 45 minutes. Pour enchilada sauce over the casserole before serving.

COOK C. Tessendore   CHIEF E. F. Wrought

Potato Chip Chicken

Of all the easy ways to prepare chicken, this method is one of the best. It isn't even necessary to add water to the baking dish, and the result is crisp and tasty.

SERVES 8 TO 10	INGREDIENTS	SERVES 4 TO 6
2 large fryers	Chicken	1 large fryer
1 cup	Butter or margarine	½ cup
2 medium pkg.	Potato chips	1 medium pkg.

Cut chicken into serving pieces. Tear a small hole in a bag of potato chips and crush chips in the bag with rolling pin until they are fine. Melt the butter, dip the chicken in butter, and then cover with potato chip crumbs. Put in a pan and bake, uncovered, at 350° for 1 hour.

Suggestion: For a more seasoned taste, try barbecued potato chips.

COOK Don Kennedy   CHIEF Edmond Friand

Enchilada Casserole

*This casserole, a specialty of the firehouse in San Fernando,
will be enjoyed by anyone who favors Mexican food.*

SERVES 10 TO 12	INGREDIENTS	SERVES 6 TO 8
2 lbs.	Ground beef	1 lb.
4 Tbs.	Shortening	2 Tbs.
2 small	Onions	1 small
2 lbs.	Cheddar cheese	1 lb.
2 No. 303 cans	Enchilada sauce	1 No. 303 can
4 doz.	Tortillas	2 doz.
2 cups	Shortening	1 cup
2 cups	Black olives	1 cup

Sauté meat in heated shortening. Chop onion, grate cheese, and
pit and chop olives. Add onion and half of cheese to meat, along
with half of the enchilada sauce, and simmer until onions are
tender. Using a separate skillet, soften tortillas by quickly dipping
each in heated shortening. Drain tortillas. Put about two tablespoons of meat filling in center of each tortilla and roll. Place
seam side down in the bottom of a baking dish or skillet. Pour
remaining enchilada sauce over them and sprinkle with remaining
cheese and olives. Bake, uncovered, at 350° for 15 to 20 minutes.

COOK Gary Riggs   CHIEF Edmond Friand

Oriental Casserole

The firehouse chef considered ease of preparation as well as economy when he sent us this recipe from Kodiak. Any of the leaner cuts of meat can be used successfully in this casserole.

SERVES 12	INGREDIENTS	SERVES 4
6 lbs.	Pork	2 lbs.
To taste	Salt and pepper	To taste
6 to 8 Tbs.	Shortening	2 to 4 Tbs.
3 cups	Celery	1 cup
3	Onions	1
3 10½-oz. cans	Golden mushroom or cream of mushroom soup	1 10½-oz. can
3 soup cans	Water	1 soup can
3 to 4 Tbs.	Soy sauce	1 to 2 Tbs.
1½ cups	Rice, uncooked	½ cup

Cut meat into bite-size cubes and season with salt and pepper. Brown meat in heated shortening in frying pan and set aside. Pour mushroom soup into a baking dish, and stir in water gradually to avoid lumps. Chop celery and onions. Add celery, onions, soy sauce, and uncooked rice to soup. Add browned meat and stir gently to evenly distribute rice and other ingredients. Cover and bake 1½ hours at 350°

COOK Charles Naughton   CHIEF George Magnusen

Filipino-Style
Chicken

SERVES 12	INGREDIENTS	SERVES 6
10 lbs.	Chicken thighs or wings	5 lbs.
8 to 10 Tbs.	Cooking oil	4 to 6 Tbs.
8 Tbs.	Vinegar	4 Tbs.
3 large	Bay leaves	2 medium
To taste	Garlic	To taste
About 20	Peppercorns	About 10
1 cup	Soy sauce	½ cup

In a skillet, add chicken pieces to the heated cooking oil, along with the vinegar, bay leaves, garlic, and peppercorns. Cook over high heat for 20 minutes. Add soy sauce and reduce heat to medium. Cover and cook until chicken is tender.

COOKS All personnel   CHIEF Charles Takeguchi

Gisantis
(Pork or Chicken with Peas)

SERVES 10	INGREDIENTS	SERVES 5
4 lbs.	Pork or chicken	2 lbs.
½ cup	Cooking oil	¼ cup
1 medium	Onion	1 small
1 large	Potato	1 medium
1 2-oz. jar	Pimentoes	1 oz.
2	Garlic cloves, crushed	1
2 8-oz. cans	Tomato sauce	1 8-oz. can
2 No. 303 cans	Peas	1 No. 303 can
To taste	Salt and pepper	To taste

Cut meat into bite-size pieces and fry in heated cooking oil until well browned. Chop the onions, potato, and pimentoes and add to the meat with the garlic and tomato sauce. Cook for 45 minutes over medium heat. Stir in peas and season with salt and pepper during last 10 minutes of cooking time.

cooks All personnel   chief Charles Takeguchi

Japanese-Style
Barbecue

SERVES 12	INGREDIENTS	SERVES 6
6 lbs.	Beefsteaks, thinly sliced	3 lbs.
1 cup	Soy sauce	½ cup
2 pieces	Ginger root, crushed	1 piece
2 Tbs.	Brown sugar	1 Tbs.
2 Tbs.	Sugar	1 Tbs.
2	Garlic cloves, crushed	1

Soak beef slices for 2 to 3 hours in marinade made from all other ingredients. Grill over hot charcoals until tender and browned.

COOKS All personnel   CHIEF Charles Takeguchi

Pork with
Sweet-Sour Sauce

Captain Akiona of the Honolulu Fire Department tells us that the men there use the cheaper cuts of meat, such as stew beef, frankfurters and hamburger, prepared a hundred different ways.

SERVES 12	INGREDIENTS	SERVES 6
4 to 5 lbs.	Lean pork	2 to 3 lbs.
To taste	Salt and pepper	To taste
To taste	MSG	To taste
2	Green peppers	1

Batter

1 cup	Flour	½ cup
½ cup	Cornstarch	¼ cup
1 tsp.	Baking powder	½ tsp.
2 Tbs.	Egg, beaten	1 Tbs.
2 tsp.	Cooking oil	1 tsp.
1 cup	Water	½ cup
For deep frying	Cooking oil	For deep frying

Sauce

⅔ cup	Catsup	⅓ cup
1½ cups	Sugar	¾ cup
1⅓ cups	Water	⅔ cup
½ tsp.	Salt	¼ tsp.
½ tsp.	MSG	¼ tsp.
2 Tbs.	Soy sauce	1 Tbs.
1 cup	Vinegar	½ cup
7 Tbs.	Cornstarch	3½ Tbs.
⅔ cup	Water	⅓ cup

Trim pork and cut into ½" cubes. Season with salt, pepper, and MSG. Cut green peppers into ½" squares. Set pork and peppers aside while preparing batter. Mix flour, cornstarch, and baking powder together. In a separate bowl, combine beaten egg, cooking oil, and water. Add these to dry ingredients. Dip pork in batter and deep fry in hot oil 3 to 5 minutes until brown. Drain cooked pieces of pork on paper towel. Arrange on platter, garnish with pepper squares and keep warm while preparing sweet-sour sauce.

Sauce: Combine catsup, sugar, water, salt, MSG, and soy sauce and bring to a boil. Add vinegar and bring to a boil again. Make a paste of cornstarch and water and add this gradually to other sauce ingredients in pan, stirring to avoid lumps. Bring to boil again and pour over cooked pork and pepper squares.

COOK Peter Akiona, Jr.   CHIEF B. K. Aiu

Index

F

Filipino-style chicken, 195
Filleted breast of goose or duck,
  112
Filling, pecan-coconut, for chocolate cake, 82
Fish. *See also* Shellfish
  bluefish baked in butter, 14
  cakes, 32
  catfish stew, 50
  chowder, 4
  crappie delight, 118
  deep-fried, 79
  flounder fillets, stuffed, 18
  salmon
    loaf, 94, 186
    steak, broiled, 182
Flatterer of the Palate, 81
Flounder fillets, stuffed, 18
40 cents' worth of peas and 7
  dollars' worth of ham, 141
Frankfurters, bite-size corn
  dogs, 155
French-cut green beans with
  sweet-sour sauce, 96
French-Italian shrimp and
  macaroni, 138
Fricassee of chicken, 144
Fritters
  clam, 185
  corn, 68
Frosting
  caramel, 67
  cocoa, 82
  fudge, 170
Frozen vanilla custard, 38
Fruit desserts
  apple crisp, 190
  apple pie, 37
  baked apples, 22

banana pudding, 55
cherry torte, 100
cream-cheese pie, 142
huckleberry upside-down cake,
  183
peach cobbler, 76
strawberries in the snow, 40
Fruit salad
  gelatine, 58, 63, 188
  with sour cream, 51
  tossed, 127
Fudge brownies, 169
Fudge frosting, 170

G

Game
  moose rolls, 119
  venison steak, 44
Garlic bread, 31
Gelatine salad
  cranberry, 188
  lime, 63
  pineapple-cheese-nut, 58
  tomato aspic, 83
German casserole, 153
German potato salad, 104
Giblet gravy for roast turkey, 66
Gisantis, 196
Goose, filleted breast of, 112
Gravy
  bulldog, for fried liver, 54
  for chicken fricassee, 144
  giblet, for roast turkey, 66
  gingersnap, for sauerbraten, 98
  for roast beef, 8, 140
  sour cream, for chicken papri-
    kash, 83
Green beans in sweet-sour sauce,
  96
Gumbo, shrimp, 146

206